PENGUIN BOOKS — GREAT IDEAS

Three Japanese Buddhist Monks

T0176227

Saigyō

1118–1190

Kamo no Chōmei

c.1155–1216

Yoshida Kenkō

c.1283–c.1352

Three Japanese Buddhist Monks

Translated by Meredith McKinney

PENGUIN BOOKS — GREAT IDEAS

PENGUIN BOOKS

UK | USA | Canada | Ireland | Australia
India | New Zealand | South Africa

Penguin Books is part of the Penguin Random House group
of companies whose addresses can be found at
global.penguinrandomhouse.com.

Essays by Chōmei and Kenkō taken from *Essays in Idleness and
Hōjoki* published in Penguin Classics 2013
This selection published in Penguin Books 2020
001

Translations copyright © Meredith McKinney, 2013, 2020

Set in 11.2/13.75 pt Dante MT Std
Typeset by Jouve (UK), Milton Keynes
Printed and bound in Great Britain by Clays Ltd, Elcograf S.p.A.

A CIP catalogue record for this book
is available from the British Library

ISBN: 978-0-241-47291-0

www.greenpenguin.co.uk

MIX
Paper from
responsible sources
FSC® C018179

Penguin Random House is committed to a
sustainable future for our business, our readers
and our planet. This book is made from Forest
Stewardship Council® certified paper.

Contents

The Monk Who Built a Hut and Meditated in the Depths of Mount Utsu

FROM *SENJŪSHŌ*

Once I went wandering along Eastern Road. Finding the cherry blossoms of Mount Utsu hard to pass by, I went searching deeper in, and along the famous vine-tangled narrow path famed from poetry of old, beneath trees so dense that sunlight failed to penetrate, I found a monk who had built a meagre hut and sat there in *zazen* meditation.

He looked around forty years of age. How and where had he come from, and what sorrow had driven him to dwell here? I asked. And what had awakened him to the Buddhist Truth?

'I am a man of the land of Sagami,' he told me. 'Born into a samurai family, I was destined to be one who carried a long sword at my side and wielded the bow and arrow – but I was stricken with fear when I understood life's transience. Though I practised meditation from time to time, stilling my mind, I was unable to leave the world behind me. Then my wife, my companion of many years, died, and my heart grew more and more determined to take that decisive step.

'And so I cut off my hair and retreated to this mountain. In the beginning I spent some time in the temple known as Matsushima, but those close to me troubled me with their fussing so I left without their knowledge, and for the past two years I have lived here.

'From time to time I go out to the local village and beg for food, and in this way I keep this meagre body and soul together. My heart is now so pure that I feel no real desire for food any more, and I eat only two or three times a month.'

Full of reverence and envy of him, I told him that I wished to live there with him. 'A foolish idea,' he replied. 'I would stray from my path; you would fall into error. We would not help each other along the Way. Wherever you go, that is where you must purify your heart. But please visit me again.' There was not such a great distance between us in fact, but I was sadly lacking in resolution, and before long I set off on my travels again and did not settle there, though I promised to return.

I had every intention of visiting him on my way back to the capital, but before I knew it I had wandered on into Oku and stayed there quite some time. On my way home again I took a different route, and although I had not forgotten him my promise remained unfulfilled.

The manner of his awakening to the Buddhist Truth was particularly pure. India and China are far-off places and I will say nothing of them here, nor have I known our own country's wise men of old. Yet it seems to me that, among the many I have seen, there is none to match the awe-inspiring nature of this man. He hid himself away in deep ravines, watching the pure moon emerge from wind-torn clouds through the pines on mountain peaks. It fills me with envy to think of it. Even to hear those occasional scraps of tales written of such people, to witness the pure serenity of such dwellings by the sea or deep among mountains, fills one's eyes with tears. How much more must he have wept for joy to live there and see such a world all around him. And how envy overwhelms me to think of him now and imagine in what Pure Land he must be dwelling.

What, then, is this form of practice called *zazen*? It is, surely, to relinquish all the objects of perception, to focus the mind on the mind, and thereby to cast away the mind. To hold in your heart such *koans* as 'The mud ox runs in the sky; the wooden horse neighs in the heavens.' And when you do, what then? You simply hold it, tirelessly. In essence, if your urge for the Buddhist truth is sincere, all ways in are one. 'Thoughts are like old mice; enlightenment is like a young cat,' as the old saying goes. To still the mind deeply and perform *zazen* is the practice of Mind, one of the three Buddhist practices, and is a greater thing than to build a million pagodas to the Buddha. Remember, all that is good must come only from the heart.

The Ten-Foot-Square Hut

CHŌMEI

On flows the river ceaselessly, nor does its water ever stay the same. The bubbles that float upon its pools now disappear, now form anew, but never endure long. And so it is with people in this world, and with their dwellings.

In our dazzling capital the houses of high and low crowd the streets, a jostling throng of roof and tile, and have done so down the generations – yet ask if this is truly so and you discover that almost no house has been there from of old. Some burned down last year and this year were rebuilt. Others were once grand mansions, gone to ruin, where now small houses stand.

And it is the same with those that live in them. The places remain, as full of people as ever, but of those one saw there once now only one or two in twenty or thirty still survive. Death in the morning, at evening another birth – this is the way of things, no different from the bubbles on the stream.

Where do they come from, these newborn? Where do the dead go? I do not know. Nor do I know why our hearts should fret over these brief dwellings, or our eyes find such delight in them. An owner and his home vie in their impermanence, as the vanishing dew upon the morning glory. The dew may disappear while the flower remains – yet it lives on only to fade with the morning sun. Or perhaps the flower wilts while the dew still lies – but though it stays, it too will be gone before the evening.

Over the more than forty rounds of seasons since I first grew conscious of the world about me, I have seen many extraordinary things.

It would have been the twenty-eighth day in the fourth month of the third year of Angen. The wind was fierce and the night tumultuous, and at the Hour of the Dog a fire broke out in the capital's south-east, and spread to the north-west. Eventually the Shujaku Gate, the Hall of State, the University Hall and the Civil Affairs Bureau all caught fire, and in a single night were reduced to ashes.

It was said the fire started in Higuchi Tominokōji, and began in a lodging house where some dancers were staying. The flames spread hither and yon on the fickle wind, fanning out wide over the city. Houses beyond were choked with smoke, while from those nearby, flames spouted and sparks rained down. Clouds of ash poured up into the sky, lit red by the fire beneath, and in the midst of all this blazing scarlet the ragged flames leaped whole blocks at a time, flying unresisting on the wind. For those caught up in the blaze, it must have seemed a nightmare. Some fell, choked with smoke;

others were blinded by the flames and quickly perished. Where others managed to escape with their life, they left behind them all their worldly goods. All those countless treasures were turned to dust and ashes. How much was lost, all told?

In this fire sixteen noble houses alone were destroyed, not to mention the countless others. It is said that fully one-third of the capital was lost. Scores of men and women died, and who knows how many horses and oxen besides?

All human undertaking is folly, but it is most particularly futile to spend your wealth and trouble your peace of mind by building a house in the perilous capital.

Again, in the fourth month of the fourth year of Jishō a great whirlwind sprang up in the Nakamikado Kyōgoku area, and swept down through the city to around Rokujō.

Over three or four blocks, every single house, large or small, in the path of the swirling wind was destroyed. Some were utterly flattened, while only the pillars and beams of others remained. The wind tore up gates and brought them down four or five blocks away. It blew away fences, making houses one with their neighbours. Needless to say, every last belonging inside the houses flew into the air, while cypress bark thatch and shingles swirled in the gale like winter leaves. The wind raised such a spiralling smoke of dust that the eye was quite blinded, and the dreadful roar drowned out all speech. The karmic wind of hell itself would be such as this, it seemed. Not only houses were damaged – countless people were hurt or maimed in trying to repair them. At length the wind moved off south-south-west, causing grief to many.

Whirlwinds are quite common, but do they ever blow like this? This was no ordinary wind, and all wondered whether it was not some portent from on high.

Also in the sixth month of the fourth year of Jishō, the capital was suddenly relocated, confounding everyone. One generally hears it said that this city has been the capital since it was so designated in the time of Emperor Saga, more than four hundred years ago. It should never have been moved arbitrarily on a casual whim like that, and it was only too natural that everyone was so distressed and anxious.

But complaints availed them nothing; everyone, from the emperor to his ministers and nobles, was obliged to move. And how could any among those in attendance at the palace choose to remain back there alone in the old capital? Those hoping to advance their rank and position, those who relied on the emperor's support, strove to make the move as soon as possible, while others, who had missed their moment, had been passed over in life and could hope for no advancement, stayed behind and grieved.

As the days passed, ruin fell upon those fine houses with their jostling throng of roofs. The buildings were dismantled and floated down the Yodo, and before our eyes the land turned to cropping fields. Tastes changed – now everyone prized only the horse and saddle, and the ox and carriage went quite unused. Now property on the south-west seaboard was sought after, while no one cared for estates to the north or east.

At around this time I happened to have reason to visit the new capital, so I went down to Settsu. Looking around, I noted that the area was too cramped to be sectioned off into proper wards. To the north the land rose steeply up to mountains, while to the south it sloped straight down to the nearby sea. There was a constant crash of waves, and a fierce offshore wind blew. The imperial palace stood back in the hills, and was rather reminiscent of how the old Log Palace might have looked, almost charming in its eccentricity.

Where could all those houses be, that had day after day been dismantled and floated downstream in such quantities that they clogged the waterways? Empty plots were everywhere, buildings were few. The old capital was now a ruin, while the new had yet to rise. Every last person felt suspended, unsettled, adrift as floating clouds. The place's former residents lamented the loss of their land. Those who had moved there bewailed the difficulties of building. Along the roads I witnessed men who should by rights travel in a carriage sitting astride a horse, and courtiers who would normally be dressed in court robes wearing instead the new *hitatare*. The old capital's ways had undergone a sudden transformation, and fashions now were indistinguishable from the uncouth country warrior's.

It is said that changes in customs presage times of

upheaval, and indeed it was so, for as the days passed all grew increasingly disturbed and restive, until at length the people's grievances bore fruit, and in the winter of that year the capital was returned to its former site. Who knows what happened to all the houses that were dismantled and taken down there, however, for many were never restored.

It is told that in the days of the wise rulers of old the land was governed with compassion – the eaves of the reed-thatched palace roofs were left untrimmed, and if the emperor saw only a thin trail of smoke rising from his people's cooking fires, he excused them payment of even the stipulated taxes. This was because these rulers were given to benevolence and service to their people. We need only compare our present age to theirs to see the difference.

Again, around the Yōwa era I believe it was, although so much time has passed that I no longer quite remember, there was a terrible two-year famine in the world. Drought in spring and summer, typhoons and floods in autumn – disaster followed on disaster, and all the crops failed. In vain did people till the fields in spring and plant in summer; autumn and winter brought no bustling harvest, no storing up of food.

All this drove people throughout the provinces to leave their land and migrate elsewhere, or desert their homes and simply take to the hills. Various prayers to the gods were instigated and fervent Buddhist ceremonies performed at the palace, but to no avail. All the capital's many activities essentially depended on the countryside, and once provisions ceased to arrive, what hope was there of keeping up even a semblance of normalcy? People were driven to offer all their treasured possessions to buyers for a song, but no one would so much as glance at them. And if any exchange did happen to be made, money meant almost nothing, while grain was everything. Beggars crowded the roadsides, and the sound of their wailing filled the ears.

So the first year drew somehow to a close. We hoped for recovery in the new year, but instead a plague was added to our woes, and every semblance of the old life was now gone. All despaired, and we were like fish in a fast-drying pond as calamity tightened its grip on the world from day to day. Finally, those who still looked reasonably presentable took to the streets, clad in hats and leggings, going from door to door, desperately begging. These miserable wretches could be seen staggering along one minute and fallen the next. Countless numbers starved to death by walls and on roadsides. None knew how to dispose of all these corpses; the air was filled with their stench, and one could only avert the eyes from the frequent sight of slowly decomposing bodies. As for the dry river bed, the bodies lay so thick that there was no room for horses and carts to pass.

The poor wood-cutters and other common folk could no longer carry wood from exhaustion, so even fuel became scarce in the city, and those who had nowhere else to turn were reduced to tearing down their own houses and selling the wood in the marketplace. It was said that the price for what a man could carry there would not even keep him alive a day. Strangely, among the wood sold for fuel one saw some with touches of cinnabar or gold leaf – on enquiry, I learned that some as a last resort were going to run-down old temples, stealing the Buddhist images, dismantling the decorative woodwork in the worship hall and breaking these up to sell. Born into these vile latter days, it has been my lot to witness such heartbreaking things.

And I saw other pitiful things besides. Where a man could not bear to part from his wife, or a woman loved her husband dearly, it was always the one whose love was the deeper who died first – in their sympathy for the other they would put themselves second, and give their partner any rare morsel that came their way. So also, if parent and child lived together the parent was always the first to die; a baby would still lie suckling, unaware that its mother was dead.

A monk by the name of Ryūgyō Hōin from Ninnaji, sorrowing to see people dying in such countless numbers, took to inscribing the sacred Sanskrit syllable 'A' on the forehead of any he met with, to lead them to rebirth in paradise. When a count was made of all the dead, the total for the fourth and fifth months came to over 42,300 in the area from Ichijō south and from Kujō north, from East Kyōgoku west and Shujaku east. Of course there were many who died before and after this time, and if all the outlying areas such as the Kamo riverbed, Shirakawa and the Nishi no Kyō were added in, the numbers would be incalculable – and how much more so with the provinces beyond!

Such things also happened, I have heard, in the reign of Emperor Sutoku back in the Chōshō era, but I know nothing of the experience of those times. What I have seen with my own eyes was certainly strange and dreadful.

Also around the same time, as I recall, there was a great earthquake, and a quite exceptional one it was. Mountainsides collapsed, damming the streams, and the sea tilted up and flooded over the land. Water gushed from the rent earth, great rocks split asunder and tumbled into the valleys below. Boats rowing offshore were tossed in the waves, while horses lost their footing on the roads. Not a single temple building or pagoda around the capital remained intact. Some collapsed, others leaned and fell. Like thick plumes of smoke, the dust rose. The roar of shuddering earth and the crash of buildings resounded like thunder. Anyone indoors was sure to be crushed, but we rushed out only to find the earth split open at our feet. Lacking wings, there could be no escaping to the air. Had we only been dragons, we might have fled to the clouds! Among all the terrors, I realized then, the most terrifying is an earthquake.

The dreadful shaking soon ceased, but the aftershocks continued for some time. Not a day passed without twenty or thirty tremors, of a strength that would normally seem startlingly strong. Finally, ten or twenty days later, the intervals between them lengthened – it would be four or five times a day, then two or three, then every second day, then once in two or three. All told, the aftershocks must have been felt for around three months.

Of the four elements, water, fire and wind commonly inflict harm, while earth causes no great disruptions. Back in the old days, perhaps in the Saikō era, there was a great earthquake that knocked off the head of the buddha of Tōdaiji Temple and caused tremendous damage, but it was not as bad as this.

At the time, all spoke of how futile everything was in the face of life's uncertainties, and their hearts seemed for a while a little less clouded by worldliness, but time passed, and now, years later, no one so much as mentions that time.

Yes, take it for all in all, this world is a hard place to live, and both we and our dwellings are fragile and impermanent, as these events reveal. And besides, there are the countless occasions when situation or circumstance cause us anguish.

Imagine you are someone of no account, who lives next to a powerful man. There may be something that deeply delights you, but you cannot go ahead and express your joy. If something has brought you terrible grief, you cannot raise your voice and weep. You worry over your least action and tremble with every move you make, like a sparrow close to a falcon's nest. Or take a poor man who lives next to a rich one. Ashamed at the sorry sight he makes, he is forever cringing obsequiously before his neighbour as he comes and goes. He must witness his wife and children and his servants filled with envy, and have to hear how the neighbour despises him, and each fresh thought will unsettle him so that he has not a moment's tranquillity.

If you live in a cramped city area, you cannot escape disaster when a fire springs up nearby. If you live in some remote place, commuting to and fro is filled with problems, and you are in constant danger from thieves. A powerful man will be beset by cravings, one without family ties will be scorned. Wealth brings great anxiety, while with poverty come fierce resentments. Dependence on others puts you in their power, while care for others will snare you in the worldly attachments of affection. Follow the social rules, and they hem you in; fail to do so, and you are thought as good as crazy.

Where can one be, what can one do, to find a little safe shelter in this world, and a little peace of mind?

I came into house and property through my paternal grandmother, and lived there for many years. Later, my ties with the place were broken, I came down in the world and, for all my fond memories, I eventually had to leave my home. Past thirty, I chose to build another little house.

It was a mere tenth the size of my former home. I built only a single dwelling for myself; there was no means to add any decent outbuildings. I managed to put a wall around it, but funds did not stretch to a front gate.

I used bamboo as the frame for a shed to hold the carriage. Things were always far from safe whenever snow fell or the wind blew. The place was near the river so was in deep danger of flooding, and robbers were a source of constant worry.

All told, I spent some thirty troubled years withstanding the vagaries of this world. At each new setback, I understood afresh how wretched my luck is. And so, in the spring of my fiftieth year, I came to leave my home and take the tonsure, and turned my back on the world. I had never had wife and children, so there were no close ties that were difficult to break. I had no rank and salary to forgo. What was there to hold me to the world? I made my bed among the clouds of Ōhara's mountains, and there I passed five fruitless years.

Now at sixty, with the dew of life about to fade, I have fashioned for myself another dwelling to hold me for these final years. I am, if you will, like a traveller who throws up a shelter for the night, or an old silkworm spinning his cocoon. It is not a hundredth the size of the house of my middle years. As I complained my way through life, each passing year has added to my age, and each move reduced my dwelling.

This house looks quite unlike a normal one. It is a mere ten feet square, and less than seven feet high. Since I was not much concerned about where I lived, I did not construct the house to fit the site. I simply set up a foundation, put up a bit of a roof and fastened each joint with a metal catch, so that if I didn't care for one place I could easily move to another. Just how much trouble would it be to rebuild, after all? The house would take a mere two cartloads to shift, and the only expense would be the carrier.

Since retiring here to Mount Hino, I have added a three-foot awning on the east side of my hut, beneath which to store firewood and cook. On the south I put up a veranda of bamboo slats, with an offerings shelf at its western end. Inside there is a standing screen dividing off the north-west section of the room, where I have set up a painted image of Amida with another of the bodhisattva Fugen hung next to it, and a copy of *The Lotus Sutra* placed before them. At the room's eastern edge I have spread a tangle of bracken to serve as bed. A shelf hangs from the ceiling in the south-west corner, holding three black leather boxes that contain extracts from the poetic anthologies, musical treatises, *Essentials of Salvation* and so forth. Beside this stand one *koto* and one *biwa*. The *koto* is the folding kind, the *biwa* has a detachable neck. Such is my temporary abode.

As for its surroundings, to the south is a bamboo water pipe, and I have placed rocks there to make a pool. The forest is close by the house, so I am not short of brushwood to gather. The name of the place is Toyama. Vines cover the paths, trees throng the nearby valley, but the land is open to the west. Indeed there are not a few aids to my meditations. In spring I gaze upon swathes of wisteria, which hang shining in the west like the purple clouds that bear the soul to heaven. In summer I hear the song of the *hototogisu*, and at each call he affirms his promise to lead me over the mountain path of death. In autumn the voice of the cricket fills my ears, a sound that seems to sorrow over a fleeting life so soon cast off. In winter, the snow fills me with pathos. The sight of it piling high only to melt and vanish is like the mounting sins that block our path to redemption, which penitence will erase.

When I tire of chanting the *nenbutsu* and feel disinclined to read the sutras, I can choose to rest and laze as I wish. There is no one to stand in my way or to shame me. Though I have taken no vow of silence, my solitude protects me from the evils of speech. I make no special effort to abide by the precepts, but with such conducive surroundings, what could lead me to break them?

On mornings when my thoughts turn to the 'white retreating waves' of this transient life, I gaze out to the boats that ply the river at Okanoya, and savour as my own the feelings of the old poet Novice Mansei. On evenings when the wind rustles in the leaves of the *katsura* trees, I cast my thoughts back to Xunyang Inlet, and pluck my *biwa* in the way of Tsunenobu. And if the mood is still upon me, often I play to the sough of wind in the pines the piece called 'Autumn Wind Music', or 'Flowing Spring' to the murmur of running water. My skill is poor, but then I do not aim to please the ears of others. I play alone, I sing alone, simply for my own fulfilment.

There is a little brushwood shack at the foot of the mountain, the home of the local warden. He has a little boy who sometimes comes to visit, and in idle hours I go off rambling with him. He is ten, I am sixty – a vast difference in age, yet we find our pleasure in the same things. We pick the seed-heads of grasses, collect rock-pear berries, gather mountain yams or pluck wild parsley. At other times we might go down to the rice fields, to glean the fallen ears of rice and sheave them up. If the day is fine we scramble up to the peak and gaze off to the skies of the capital, my old home, or look out over Mount Kohata, Fushimi Village, Toba and Hatsukashi. No one owns a splendid view, so nothing prevents the heart's delight in it.

If the walk is not too much for me, and I feel inclined to go further afield, I follow the ridgeline over Mount Sumi and Kasadori to pay my respects at Iwama or Ishiyama Temples. At other times, I might go on over the plain of Awazu to call on Semimaru's old site, or cross Tanakami River to visit the grave of Sarumaro. On my way back, depending on the season, I may linger over the cherry blossoms, search out the autumn leaves, pluck young fern shoots or gather nuts as I go, as offerings for the altar or as gifts to take home.

On quiet nights, the moon at my window recalls to me past friends, and tears wet my sleeve at the cries of the monkeys. The fireflies in the nearby grass blend their little lights with the fishermen's fires of distant Makinoshima; the sound of dawn rain comes to me like a storm wind in the treetops. When I hear the soft cry of the pheasant, it seems to me my own father or mother; the mountain deer that have learned to come so close reveal to me how distant from the world I have become.

There are times when I stir the embers of my fire to keep me company in the wakefulness of old age. There is nothing to fear from this mountain – the owl's cry is poignant to my ears, and through the seasons I never tire of the mountain's moving beauties. And for one who thought and understood more deeply still than I, this place would surely hold yet greater joys.

When I first came to live here, I thought my time would be brief, but already five years have passed. This passing shelter of mine has slowly become a home; the eaves are deep in rotting leaves, moss covers the foundations.

When news of the capital happens to come my way, I learn of many people in high places who have met their end since I retired to this mountain, and other lesser folk besides, too many to be told. And how many houses, too, have been lost in all those fires? In all this, my mere passing shelter has remained tranquil and safe from fears.

Small it may be, but there is a bed to sleep on at night, and a place to sit in the daytime. As a simple place to house myself, it lacks nothing. The hermit crab prefers a little shell for his home. He knows what the world holds. The osprey chooses the wild shoreline, and this is because he fears mankind. And I too am the same. Knowing what the world holds and its ways, I desire nothing from it, nor chase after its prizes. My one craving is to be at peace, my one pleasure to live free of troubles.

People do not always build a house with the important

things in mind. Some will build for wife and children or for the wider household, others for their intimates and friends. Some may build for their master or their teacher, or even for their possessions or their oxen and horses. But I have built this house for my own self and for no one else. And this is because, the world being what it is, and the way I am now, I have no one who shares my life, nor any servants to work for me. Who would I put in a larger house if I built one, after all?

People who cultivate friendships prize men with wealth, and prefer those who are eager to please. They do not always cherish friends who are loving, or pure of heart. Best by far is the company of flute and strings, and of the flowers and moon. Servants and retainers crave endless rewards, and love a master who showers them with favours. They have no interest in affectionate concern or a calm and peaceful life. Better far to be your own servant. How? If something needs doing, use yourself to do it. It may be tiring, but it is easier than employing another and troubling yourself over him. If you need to go somewhere, walk yourself. You may grow weary, but better far than worrying over horse and saddle, oxen and cart.

These days, I divide myself into two uses – these hands are my servants, these feet my transport. They serve me just as I wish. Mind knows when things feel hard for the body; at such times it will grant the body rest, and work it when it is willing. Yet, work the body though it does, the mind will never push too far, and if the body is reluctant, this will not perturb the mind.

Indeed the habit of walking and working is good for the health. Why sit idly about, after all? It is a sin to bring trouble to others. Why should I borrow another's strength?

So too with food and clothing. Be it robe of vine fibre or hempen quilt, I cover myself in whatever comes to hand, and keep myself alive with wild asters from the fields and nuts from the mountains. Since I do not mix with others, shame causes me no regrets. Plain fare tastes all the better when food is scarce.

I do not make claims for these pleasures to disparage the rich. I am simply comparing my past life with my present one. The Triple World is solely Mind. Without a peaceful mind, elephants, horses and the seven treasures are worthless things, palaces and fine towers mean nothing.

I love my tiny hut, my lonely dwelling. When I chance to go down into the capital, I am ashamed of my lowly beggar status, but once back here again I pity those who chase after the sordid rewards of the world. If any doubt my words, let them look to the fish and the birds. Fish never tire of water, a state incomprehensible to any but the fish. The bird's desire for the forest makes sense to none but birds. And so it is with the pleasure of seclusion. Who but one who lives it can understand its joys?

Like the moon that hangs above the mountain rim, my life now tilts towards its close. Soon I will enter the darkness of the Three Paths. What point is there in mulling over past actions?

The Buddha's essential teaching is to relinquish all attachment. This fondness for my hut I now see must be error, and my attachment to a life of seclusion and peace is an impediment to rebirth. How could I waste my days like this, describing useless pleasures?

In the quiet dawn I ponder this, and question my own heart: you fled the world to live among forest and mountain in order to discipline the mind and practise the Buddhist Way. But though you have all the trappings of a holy man, your heart is corrupt. Your dwelling may aspire to be the hut of the holy Vimilakīrti himself, but the practice you maintain in it cannot match even that of the fool Śuddhipanthaka. Have you after all let the poverty ordained by past sins distract you? Or have your delusions tipped you over into madness?

When I confront my heart thus, it cannot reply. At most, this mortal tongue can only end in three faltering invocations of the holy, unapproachable name of Amida.

*Written in his hut on Toyama at the close of the third month in the second year of Kenryaku, by the monk Ren'in.**

---

* Ren'in was the Buddhist name of Kamo no Chōmei.

How Will You Spend Your Last Day?

KENKŌ

To be born into this world of ours, it seems, brings with it so much to long for.

The rank of emperor is, of course, unspeakably exalted; even his remotest descendants fill one with awe, having sprung from no mere human seed.

Needless to say, the great ruler, and even the lesser nobles who are granted attendant guards to serve them, are also thoroughly magnificent. Their children and grandchildren too are still impressive, even if they have come down in the world. As for those of lesser degree, although they may make good according to their rank, and put on airs and consider themselves special, they are really quite pathetic.

No one could be less enviable than a monk. Sei Shōnagon wrote that people treat them like unfeeling lumps of wood, and this is perfectly true. And there is nothing impressive about the way those with power will throw their weight around. As the holy man Sōga, I think, remarked, fame and fortune are an affliction for a monk, and violate the Buddha's teachings.

There is much to admire, though, in a dedicated recluse.

It is most important to present well, in both appearance and bearing. One never tires of spending time with someone whose speech is attractive and pleasing to the ear, and who does not talk overmuch. There is nothing worse than when someone you thought impressive reveals himself as lacking in sensibility. Status and personal appearance are things one is born with, after all, but surely the inner man can always be improved with effort. It is a great shame to see a fine upstanding fellow fall in with low and ugly types who easily run rings round him, and all for want of cultivation and learning.

A man should learn the orthodox literature, write poetry in Chinese as well as Japanese, and study music, and should ideally also be a model to others in his familiarity with ceremonial court customs and precedents. He should write a smooth, fair hand, carry the rhythm well when songs are sung at banquets, and when offered sake, make a show of declining it but nevertheless be able to drink.

★

It is an admirable thing in a man to keep his mind on the world to come, and remain heedful of the Buddhist path.

★

A man who meets with misfortune and sorrow should not shave his head and become a monk on impulse; he does better to quietly shut his gate and seclude himself unobtrusively, expecting nothing of each passing day.

Counsellor Akimoto is reputed to have wished to 'gaze upon the moon in blameless exile'. Precisely so.

★

If our life did not fade and vanish like the dews of Adashino's graves or the drifting smoke from Toribe's burning grounds, but lingered on for ever, how little the world would move us. It is the ephemeral nature of things that makes them wonderful.

Among all living creatures, it is man that lives longest. The brief dayfly dies before evening; summer's cicada knows neither spring nor autumn. What a glorious luxury it is to taste life to the full for even a single year. If you constantly regret life's passing, even a thousand long years will seem but the dream of a night.

Why cling to a life which cannot last for ever, only to arrive at ugly old age? The longer you live, the greater your share of shame. It is most seemly to die before forty at the latest. Once past this age, people develop an urge to mix with others without the least shame at their own unsightliness; they spend their dwindling years fussing adoringly over their children and grandchildren, hoping to live long enough to see them make good in the world. Their greed for the things of this world grows ever deeper, till they lose all ability to be moved by life's pathos, and become really quite disgraceful.

★

Though a home is of course merely a transient habitation, a place that is set up in beautiful taste to suit its owner is a delightful thing.

Even the moonlight is so much the more moving when it shines into a house where a refined person dwells in tranquil elegance. There is nothing fashionable or showy about the place, it is true, yet the grove of trees is redolent of age, the plants in the carefully untended garden carry a hint of delicate feelings, while the veranda and open-weave fence are tastefully done, and inside the house the casually disposed things have a tranquil, old-fashioned air. It is all most refined.

How ugly and depressing to see a house that has employed a bevy of craftsmen to work everything up to a fine finish, where all the household items set out for proud display are rare and precious foreign or Japanese objects, and where even the plants in the garden are clipped and contorted rather than left to grow as they will. How could anyone live for long in such a place? The merest glimpse will provoke the thought that all this could go up in smoke in an instant.

Yes, on the whole you can tell a great deal about the owner from his home.

The Later Tokudaiji Minister once had rope strung

over the roof of the main house to stop the kites from roosting on it. 'What could be wrong with having kites on your roof? This shows what manner of man he is!' exclaimed the poet-monk Saigyō, and it is said he never called there again. I was reminded of this story when I noticed once that Prince Ayanokōji had laid rope over his Kosaka residence. Someone told me, however, that it was because he pitied the frogs in his pond when he observed how crows gathered on the roof to catch them. I was most impressed. Perhaps the Tokudaiji Minister too might have had some such reason for acting as he did?

★

One day in the tenth month, I went to call on someone in a remote mountain village beyond Kurusuno.

Making my way along the mossy path, I came at length to the lonely hut where he lived. There was not a sound except for the soft drip of water from a bamboo pipe buried deep in fallen leaves. The vase on the altar shelf with its haphazard assortment of chrysanthemums and sprigs of autumn leaves bespoke someone's presence.

Moved, I said to myself, 'One could live like this' – but my mood was then somewhat spoiled by noticing at the far end of the garden a large mandarin tree, branches bowed with fruit, that was firmly protected by a stout fence. If only that tree weren't there! I thought.

What happiness to sit in intimate conversation with someone of like mind, warmed by candid discussion of the amusing and fleeting ways of this world . . . but such a friend is hard to find, and instead you sit there doing your best to fit in with whatever the other is saying, feeling deeply alone.

There is some pleasure to be had from agreeing with the other in general talk that interests you both, but it's better if he takes a slightly different position from yours. 'No, I can't agree with that,' you'll say to each other combatively, and you'll fall into arguing the matter out. This sort of lively discussion is a pleasant way to pass the idle hours, but in fact most people tend to grumble about things different from oneself, and though you can put up with the usual boring platitudes, such men are far indeed from the true friend after your own heart, and leave you feeling quite forlorn.

★

It is a most wonderful comfort to sit alone beneath a lamp, book spread before you, and commune with someone from the past whom you have never met.

As to books – those moving volumes of *Wenxuan*, the *Wenji* of Bai Juyi, the words of Laozi and *Zhuangzi*. There are many moving works from our own land, too, by scholars of former times.

★

Going on a journey, whatever the destination, makes you feel suddenly awake and alive to everything.

There are so many new things to see in rustic places and country villages as you wander about looking. It is also delightful to send word to those back home in the capital asking for news, and adding reminders to be sure and see to this or that matter.

In such places, you are particularly inclined to be attentive to all you see. You even notice the fine quality of things you've brought with you, and someone's artistic talents or beauty will delight you more than they usually would.

Withdrawing quietly to a retreat at a temple or shrine is also delightful.

★

When you are on a retreat at a mountain temple, concentrating on your devotions, the hours are never tedious, and the heart feels cleansed and purified.

★

It is an excellent thing to live modestly, shun luxury and wealth and not lust after fame and fortune. Rare has been the wise man who was rich.

In China once there was a man by the name of Xu

You, who owned nothing and even drank directly from his cupped hands. Seeing this, someone gave him a 'singing gourd' to use as a cup; he hung it in a tree, but when he heard it singing in the wind one day he threw it away, annoyed by the noise it made, and went back to drinking his water from his hands. What a free, pure spirit!

Sun Chen had no bedclothes to sleep under in the winter months, only a bundle of straw which he slept in at night and put away again each morning.

The Chinese wrote these stories to hand down to later times because they found them so impressive. No one bothers to tell such tales in our country.

*

The changing seasons are moving in every way.

Everyone seems to feel that 'it is above all autumn that moves the heart to tears', and there is some truth in this, yet surely it is spring that stirs the heart more profoundly. Then, birdsong is full of the feel of spring, the plants beneath the hedges bud into leaf in the warm sunlight, the slowly deepening season brings soft mists, while the blossoms at last begin to open, only to meet with ceaseless winds and rain that send them flurrying restlessly to earth. Until the leaves appear on the boughs, the heart is endlessly perturbed.

The scented flowering orange is famously evocative, but it is above all plum blossom that has the power to carry you back to moments of cherished memory. The exquisite kerria, the hazy clusters of wisteria blossom – all these things linger in the heart.

Someone has said that at the time of the Buddha's birthday and the Kamo festival in the fourth month, when the trees are cool with luxuriant new leaf, one is particularly moved by the pathos of things and by a longing for others, and indeed it is true. And who could not be touched to melancholy in the fifth month, when the sweet flag iris leaves are laid on roofs, and the rice seedlings are planted out, and the water rail's knocking call is heard? The sixth month is also moving, with white evening-glory blooming over the walls of poor dwellings, and the smoke from smouldering smudge fires. The purifications of the sixth month are also delightful.

The festival of Tanabata is wonderfully elegant. Indeed so many things happen together in autumn – the nights grow slowly more chill, wild geese come crying over, and when the bush clover begins to yellow the early rice is harvested and hung to dry. The morning after a typhoon has blown through is also delightful.

Writing this, I realize that all this has already been spoken of long ago in *The Tale of Genji* and *The Pillow Book* – but that is no reason not to say it again. After all, things thought but left unsaid only fester inside you. So I let my brush run on like this for my own foolish solace; these pages deserve to be torn up and discarded, after all, and are not something others will ever see.

To continue – the sight of a bare wintry landscape is almost as lovely as autumn. It is delightful to see fallen autumn leaves scattered among the plants by the water's edge, or vapour rising from the garden stream on a morning white with frost. It is also especially moving to observe everyone bustling about at year's end, preparing for the new year. And then there is the forlornly touching sight of the waning moon around the twentieth day, hung in a clear, cold sky, although people consider it too dreary to look at. The Litany of Buddha Names and the Presentation of Tributes are thoroughly moving and magnificent, and in fact all the numerous court ceremonies and events at around this time, taking place as they do amidst the general end-of-year bustle, present an impressive sight. The way the Worship of the Four Directions follows so quickly upon the Great Demon Expulsion is wonderful too.

In the thick darkness of New Year's Eve, people light pine torches and rush about, so fast that their feet virtually skim the ground, making an extraordinary racket for some reason, and knocking on everyone's doors until late at night – but then at last around dawn all grows quiet, and you savour the touching moment of saying farewell to the old year. I was moved to find that in the East they still perform the ritual for dead souls on the night when the dead are said to return, although these days this has ceased to be done in the capital.

And so, watching the new year dawn in the sky, you are stirred by a sense of utter newness, although the sky looks no different from yesterday's. It is also touching to see the happy sight of new year pines gaily decorating the houses all along the main streets.

★

A certain recluse monk once remarked, 'I have relinquished all that ties me to the world, but the one thing that still haunts me is the beauty of the sky.' I can quite see why he would feel this.

★

You can find solace for all things by looking at the moon. Someone once declared that there is nothing more delightful than the moon, while another disagreed, claiming that dew is the most moving – a charming debate. Surely there is nothing that isn't moving, in fact, depending on circumstance.

Not only the moon and blossoms, but the wind in particular can stir people's hearts.

The sight of a clear stream breaking against rocks is always delightful, whatever the season.

I was truly moved when I read the words of the Chinese poem that run, 'Day and night, the Yuan and Xiang go flowing ever east, / never pausing for a grieving man.' Then there is Xi Kang, who wrote how, roving among mountain and stream, his heart delighted to see the fish and birds. Nothing provides such balm for the heart as wandering somewhere far from the world of men, in a place of pure water and fresh leaf.

★

The seclusion of the high priestess at Nonomiya was a most refined and delightful thing. It is also interesting that she must avoid Buddhist words such as 'sutra' or 'the Buddha', replacing them with 'child within' and 'dyed paper'.

All shrines to the gods have a compelling air of refinement. There is something quite special about the sight of the venerable old shrine groves, and the sacred fences surrounding the shrines themselves, and the way sacred paper streamers are tied to the boughs of the *sakaki* tree, are quite splendid.

The most delightful shrines are: Ise, Kamo, Kasuga, Hirano, Sumiyoshi, Miwa, Kibune, Yoshida, Ōharano, Matsuo and Umenomiya.

*

This world is changeable as the deeps and shallows of Asuka River – time passes, what was here is gone, joy and grief visit by turns, once splendid places change to abandoned wastelands, and even the same house as of old is now home to different people. The peach and the plum tree utter nothing – with whom can we speak of past things? Still more moving in its transience is the ruin of some fine residence of former times, whose glory we never saw.

It is deeply poignant to see the Kyōgoku-dono and Hōjōji Temple, and witness there the hopes of the man who built them, now so transfigured. The Midōdono created these magnificent buildings and donated many of his estates to the temple, full of plans that his family would continue to act as regents for future emperors and retain its worldly power – could he have dreamed then that an age would come when all that he had set up would lie in such ruin? The temple gates and the Kondō were still standing until recently, but the south gate burned in the Shōwa era. The Kondō later collapsed, and no attempt has been made to rebuild it. Only the Muryōju Hall still stands in its former state, with inside it an awe-inspiring row of nine fifteen-foot-tall images of the Buddha. It is moving, too, to see the calligraphy by Grand Counsellor Kōzei and the doors with Kaneyuki's writing, still clearly visible. The Hokke-dō is apparently still standing as well. For how much longer, I wonder?

In places where such remnants no longer exist, one can sometimes still see foundation stones in the ground, but none now know what buildings these once were.

And so we see how fickle is the world in all things, for those who would plan for a time they will not live to see.

★

How mutable the flower of the human heart, a fluttering blossom gone before the breeze's touch – so we recall the bygone years when the heart of another was our close companion, each dear word that stirred us then still unforgotten; and yet, it is the way of things that the beloved should move into worlds beyond our own, a parting far sadder than from the dead. Thus did Mozi grieve over a white thread that the dye would alter for ever, and at the crossroads Yang Zhu lamented the path's parting ways.

In Retired Emperor Horikawa's collection of one hundred poems, we read:

Where once I called on her	*mukashi mishi*
the garden fence is now in ruins –	*imo ga kakine wa*
flowering there I find	*arenikeri*
only wild violets, woven through	*tsubana majiri no*
with rank spring grasses.	*sumire nomi shite*

Such is the desolate scene that once must have met the poet's eye.

*

At times of quiet contemplation, my one irresistible emotion is an aching nostalgia for all things past.

Everyone is hushed and sleeping, and you are beguiling yourself through the long night hours by tidying away this and that, discarding bits of used writing paper you don't want to keep, when you come upon a page that someone long since dead has used for writing practice or to sketch something, and you suddenly feel yourself back inside that moment. Even if it is a long-ago letter from someone still alive, it is moving to ponder when and in what year you received it.

How melancholy to think that your own familiar

things, too, will remain in existence down the years to come, indifferent and unchanged.

★

Nothing is sadder than the aftermath of a death.

How trying it is to be jammed in together in some cramped and inconvenient mountain establishment for the forty-nine-day mourning period, performing the services for the dead. Never have the days passed faster. On the final day everyone is gruff and uncommunicative; each becomes engrossed in the importance of his own tidying and packing, then all go their separate ways. Once home again, the family will face all manner of fresh sorrows.

People go about warning each other of the various things that should be ritually avoided for the sake of the family. What a way to talk, at such a time! Really, what a wretched thing the human heart is!

Even with the passage of time the deceased is in no way forgotten, of course, but 'the dead grow more distant with each day', as the saying goes. And so, for all the memories, it seems our sorrow is no longer as acute as at death, for we begin to chatter idly and laugh again.

The corpse is buried on some deserted mountainside, we visit it only at the prescribed times, and soon moss has covered the grave marker, the grave is buried under fallen leaves, and only the howling evening winds and the moon at night come calling there.

It is all very well while there are those who remember

and mourn the dead, but soon they too pass away; the descendants only know of him by hearsay, so they are hardly likely to grieve over his death. Finally, all ceremonies for him cease, no one any longer knows who he was or even his name, and only the grasses of each passing spring grow there to move the sensitive to pity; at length even the graveyard pine that sobbed in stormy winds is cut for firewood before its thousand years are up, the ancient mound is levelled by the plough, and the place becomes a field. The last trace of the grave itself has finally disappeared. It is sad to think of.

*

One morning after a beautiful fall of snow, I had reason to write a letter to an acquaintance, but I omitted to make any mention of the snow. I was delighted when she responded, 'Do you expect me to pay any attention to the words of someone so perverse that he fails to enquire how I find this snowy landscape? What deplorable insensitivity!'

The lady is no longer alive, so I treasure even this trifling memory.

*

Around the twentieth day of the ninth month, someone invited me along to view the moon with him. We wandered and gazed until first light. Along the way, my companion came upon a house he remembered. He had his name announced, and in he went. In the unkempt and dew-drenched garden, a hint of casual incense lingered in the air. It was all movingly redolent of a secluded life.

In due course my companion emerged, but the elegance of the scene led me to stay a little longer and watch from the shadows. Soon the double doors opened a fraction wider; it seemed the lady was gazing at the moon. It would have been very disappointing had she immediately bolted the doors as soon as the visit was over. She could not know that someone would still be watching. Such sensibility could only be the fruit of a habitual attitude of mind.

I heard that this lady died not long after.

★

It is foolish to be in thrall to fame and fortune, engaged in painful striving all your life with never a moment of peace and tranquillity.

Great wealth will drive you to neglect your own well-being in pursuit of it. It is asking for harm and tempting trouble. Though you leave behind at your death a mountain of gold high enough to prop up the North Star itself, it will only cause problems for those who come after you. Nor is there any point in all those pleasures that delight the eyes of fools. Big carriages, fat horses, glittering gold and jewels – any man of sensibility would view such things as gross stupidity. Toss your gold away in the mountains; hurl your jewels into the deep. Only a complete fool is led astray by avarice.

Everyone would like to leave their name unburied for posterity – but the high-born and exalted are not necessarily fine people, surely. A dull, stupid person can be born into a good house, attain high status thanks to opportunity and live in the height of luxury, while many wonderfully wise and saintly men choose to remain in lowly positions, and end their days without ever having met with good fortune. A fierce craving for high status and position is next in folly to the lust for fortune.

We long to leave a name for our exceptional wisdom and sensibility – but when you really think about it, desire for a good reputation is merely revelling in the praise of others. Neither those who praise us nor those who denigrate will remain in the world for long, and others who hear their opinions will be gone in short order as well. Just who should we feel ashamed before, then? Whose is the recognition we should crave? Fame in fact attracts abuse and slander. No, there is nothing to be gained from leaving a lasting name. The lust for fame is the third folly.

Let me now say a few words, however, to those who dedicate themselves to the search for knowledge and the desire for understanding. Knowledge leads to deception; talent and ability only serve to increase earthly desires. Knowledge acquired by listening to others or through study is not true knowledge. So what then should we call knowledge? Right and wrong are simply part of a single continuum. What should we call good? One who is truly wise has no knowledge or virtue, nor honour nor fame. Who then will know of him, and speak of him to others? This is not because he hides his virtue and pretends foolishness – he is beyond all distinctions such as wise and foolish, gain and loss.

I have been speaking of what it is to cling to one's delusions and seek after fame and fortune. All things of this phenomenal world are mere illusion. They are worth neither discussing nor desiring.

★

Someone asked the holy priest Hōnen how to prevent himself from being negligent in his practice by inadvertently nodding off when chanting the *nenbutsu*. 'Chant for as long as you are awake,' answered Hōnen. Venerably spoken.

Likewise, Hōnen once said, 'If you are certain of entering paradise at death, your rebirth there is certain. If you are in doubt, your rebirth will be likewise.' This also was venerably said.

He also said, 'Even if you doubt, recite the *nenbutsu* and you will attain rebirth in paradise.' This too was wonderfully spoken.

★

When I went to see the horse racing at the Kamo Shrine on the fifth day of the fifth month, the view from our carriage was blocked by a throng of common folk. We all got down and moved towards the fence for a better view, but that area was particularly crowded and we couldn't make our way through.

We then noticed a priest who had climbed a chinaberry tree across the way to sit in its fork and watch from there. He was so sleepy as he clung there that he kept nodding off, and only just managed to start awake in time to save himself from falling each time. Those who saw him couldn't believe their eyes. 'What an extraordinary fool!' they all sneered. 'How can a man who's perched up there so precariously among the branches relax so much that he falls asleep?'

A thought suddenly occurred to me. 'Any of us may die from one instant to the next,' I said, 'and in fact we are far more foolish than this priest – here we are, contentedly watching the world go by, oblivious to death.'

'That's so true,' said those in front of me. 'It's really very stupid, isn't it,' and they turned around and invited me in and made room for me.

Anyone can have this sort of insight, but at that particular moment it came as a shock, which is no doubt why people were so struck by it. Humans are not mere insensate beings like trees or rocks, after all, and on occasion things can really strike home.

*

One day at the close of spring, when the air is soft and exquisite, you happen upon the house of someone who is evidently of some distinction. The place is large, with an ancient grove of trees, and cherry blossoms drift down in the garden. Unable simply to pass by, you slip into the grounds. The lattice shutters along the southern wall are all lowered, lending it a forlorn air, but you peep in through a torn blind at a half-open door in the eastern wall, and see a handsome youth of around twenty sitting there, relaxed but casually elegant, intent on a book that lies spread on the desk before him.

You long to ask someone who he might have been.

★

From a rough-woven bamboo door a very young man sets forth, tellingly clothed in glowing courtly hunting costume of a colour made indeterminate by moonlight, and deep violet gathered trousers. Accompanied by a little child attendant, he makes his way along a narrow path that winds on through the fields, drenched in dew from the brushing rice plants, and as he goes he plays quite marvellously upon a flute. No one in these parts could appreciate such playing, you think, and intrigued by the scene you follow him, wondering where he might be going. The playing ceases, and he enters the gateway of a noble house at the foot of a hill. Ox carriages stand about, propped on their empty shafts, an arresting sight in this country setting, and you ask one of the servants what is happening. 'Prince Such-and-such is in residence at the moment,' he replies, 'and I believe he is holding a Buddhist service.'

Monks are making their way towards the worship hall. A penetrating scent of incense comes wafting on the chill night breeze. Gentlewomen come and go along the roofed gallery between the main house and the worship hall, the fragrance of their scented robes drifting in their wake – such careful elegance, deep in the country where no eyes could see them.

From the wild and untrimmed 'rough autumn fields' of the garden, heavy with dripping dew and shrill with the plaint of insects, comes the murmur of a garden stream, while the clouds seem to scud more rapidly across the sky than in the city, the moon slipping in and out unpredictably among them.

★

Do not wait until old age is upon you before taking up religious practice. Most graves of the past hold men who died young.

It may be only when unexpected illness has overtaken you and you are soon to leave this world that you become aware for the first time of past error. By 'error' I mean, quite simply, taking your time over what should be accomplished swiftly, and rushing into what should be dealt with slowly. Regret fills you, but there is no point in repenting now.

You must cling to the certain knowledge that death presses in on us, and never for an instant forget it. If you do this, the corruptions of the world will surely fade from your life, and you will of necessity dedicate yourself in earnest to the Buddhist Way.

In his treatise *The Ten Causes*, Zenrin wrote of a holy man who one day was visited by someone on business that concerned them both. 'There's something urgent I must attend to,' he responded. 'It is almost upon me.' He thereupon blocked his ears, began to recite the *nenbutsu*, and before long was carried into paradise.

The holy man Shinkai was so deeply aware of the transience of this world that he would never relax and sit comfortably, but only ever squatted at the ready.

*

Houses should be built with summer chiefly in mind. One can live anywhere in winter, but a house that is ill-suited to hot weather is unbearable.

Deep water is not cooling to the eye. Shallow, running water is far cooler.

A room with a sliding door makes things brighter than one with wooden shutters, and so is better for looking closely at something.

A high ceiling is cold in winter, and darkens the lamplight.

I recall a discussion where all agreed that including areas of no particular use when making a building creates visual interest, and they can be made to serve all sorts of purposes.

'Where you live has no bearing on your dedication to the Way,' some claim. 'What's so difficult about praying for rebirth in paradise while you live in a household and have daily dealings with others?'

Only someone with no understanding of salvation in the next world would say this. If you really do hold this world to be a brief and fleeting place, and dedicate yourself to transcending its suffering, what pleasure could you find in serving your master day in day out, or busying yourself with the concerns of your family? The human heart is easily influenced; without quiet and tranquillity it is hard to pursue a practice of the Way.

These days, people are not made of the stuff of the old ascetics. If they retreat to the wilds of mountain and forest, they nevertheless eat enough to save themselves from starvation, and they cannot get by without some protection from the storms. It is only natural, then, that they should sometimes tend towards worldly desire. But this is absolutely no reason to conclude, 'There's no point in retreating from the world. Just look what happened. Why did he bother even trying?' After all, even if someone who has turned his back on the world and embarked on a practice does still harbour desires, they cannot compare with the lusts of those in powerful places. How much does it cost others to provide him with paper bedding, a hemp robe, a bowl and a meal of rough gruel? Surely his needs are simple, and his heart easily satisfied? For all his occasional urges, shame at his appearance will keep him away from evil temptation and turn him constantly towards good.

The testament to our birth in the human realm should be a strong urge to escape from this world. Surely there can be nothing to distinguish us from the beasts, if we simply devote ourselves to greed and never turn our hearts to the Buddhist Truth.

★

Those who feel the impulse to pursue the path of enlightenment should immediately take the step, and not defer it while they attend to all the other things on their mind. If you say to yourself, 'Let's just wait until after this is over,' or 'While I'm at it I'll just see to that,' or 'People will criticize me about such-and-such so I should make sure it's all dealt with and causes no problem later,' or 'There's been time enough so far, after all, and it won't take long just to a wait a little longer while I do this. Let's not rush into things,' one imperative thing after another will occur to detain you. There will be no end to it all, and the day of decision will never come.

In general, I find that reasonably sensitive and intelligent people will pass their whole life without taking the step they know they should. Would anyone with a fire close behind him choose to pause before fleeing? In a matter of life and death, one casts aside shame, abandons riches and runs. Does mortality wait on our choosing? Death comes upon us more swiftly than fire or flood. There is no escaping it. Who at that moment can refuse to part with all they love – aged parents, beloved children, lord and master, or the love of others?

★

At Shinjōin Temple there once lived a wonderfully learned high-ranking priest named Jōshin, who loved to eat taro roots. He ate them in vast amounts. Even when delivering a sermon, he would always have a dish piled high with taro by his knee, and eat while he read. Whenever he was ill, he would retire to his room for a week or a fortnight 'for treatment', and gorge himself to his heart's content on personally chosen taro of the finest quality. This is how he cured every illness. He never gave any to anyone else to eat. He ate them all himself.

Jōshin was extremely poor, but his teacher on his deathbed bequeathed to him the sum of two hundred *kan* plus monks' living quarters. He sold the building for one hundred *kan*, and dedicated the combined sum of 30,000 *hiki* to the purchase of taro. He gave this money to an acquaintance in the city for safekeeping, and drew out ten *kan* at a time to keep himself well supplied with taro. This was all he used the money for, and eventually it was all gone. 'What extraordinary piety,' everyone said, 'to come by three hundred *kan* when he was so poor, and choose to use it like this.'

Jōshin once gave the nickname 'Shiroururi' to a monk he saw. 'What does that mean?' everyone asked, to which he replied, 'I've no idea. But if such a thing existed, I believe it would look like this fellow's face.'

Jōshin was not only handsome but physically strong, a great eater, and excelled in calligraphy, scholarship and oratory. He was a leading light in the sect, and was of course valued highly in his own temple as well. However, he was an eccentric who placed little value on the world, went his own way in all things and never deferred to others.

At banquets after mass sutra readings, he wouldn't wait for all the others to be served but set in to eat as soon as his own meal was before him; then, when he wanted to leave, he simply got to his feet by himself and went off. He never ate at the prescribed times like everyone else, but whenever he wanted, be it the middle of the night or at dawn; if he felt sleepy he would retire to bed whatever the time of day, and pay no attention to others' entreaties no matter how important the occasion. Once awake, however, he would stay up without sleep for nights on end, wandering serenely about humming to himself. Yet for all his extraordinary ways he wasn't disliked, and was given free rein to do as he wanted. It must have been on account of his great virtue.

★

Stories that get passed around are for the most part lies, no doubt because the truth is so boring. People will exaggerate the facts in their telling, and with the distance of time and place they will feel increasingly free to tell a story in any way they choose; then it gets written down, and this becomes the received version.

The impressive feats of someone skilled in one of the arts will be reported as nothing short of miraculous by ignorant fools who know nothing of the art in question, while those who do know won't believe a word of it. Things witnessed are never the same as the rumour of them.

If the speaker lets his words run away with him without bothering to disguise their falsehood, his listeners will soon realize there is no truth in what he says. If someone repeats a story he himself guesses is untrue, nose twitching in self-satisfied pleasure, it is not his own lie he is telling but another's. More alarming is a fabrication told by someone quite convincingly, with a few of the details plausibly blurred, hinting that he's not quite sure of all the facts, yet in a way that makes perfect sense of the story.

People will not take much issue with an invented tale if it shows them in a good light.

When everyone is enjoying someone's free embellishment of a story, you can't very well be the only one who points out that that wasn't actually how it happened, and as you listen you may even find yourself drawn in as confirming witness, and end up helping to establish this version as fact.

Yes, one way and another, this world is full of lies. The only safe approach is to treat everything you hear as completely normal and unremarkable.

The tales told by common folk are simply astonishing to hear. People of refinement never tell tales of the strange and marvellous. Nevertheless, this does not mean one should necessarily disbelieve the stories of the miraculous powers of the gods and buddhas, or legends of their manifesting in earthly form. It is foolish to be credulous of all the tall tales people tell about such things, but there is no point in doubting everything you hear either. As a rule, you should accept such stories at face value, neither believing everything nor ridiculing it all as nonsense.

★

We swarm like ants, scurrying to east and west, dashing to north and south, folk of high birth and of low, old and young, some going, others returning, sleeping at night, rising again next morning . . . What is all this busyness? There is no end to our greed for life, our lust for gain.

We tend our bodies – to what end? Old age and death are the only sure things awaiting us. Swiftly they come, without an instant's pause. What pleasure is to be found while we await them?

The deluded have no fear of this truth. In thrall to the lure of fame and fortune, they never pause to see what lies so close before them. Fools mourn it. In their longing for eternal life, they have no understanding of the law of mutability.

What kind of man will feel depressed at being idle? There is nothing finer than to be alone with nothing to distract you.

If you follow the ways of the world, your heart will be drawn to its sensual defilements and easily led astray; if you go among people, your words will be guided by others' responses rather than come from the heart. There is nothing firm or stable in a life spent between larking about together and quarrelling, exuberant one moment, aggrieved and resentful the next. You are forever pondering pros and cons, endlessly absorbed in questions of gain and loss. And on top of delusion comes drunkenness, and in that drunkenness you dream.

Scurrying and bustling, heedless and forgetful – such are all men. Even if you do not yet understand the True Way, you can achieve what could be termed temporary happiness at least by removing yourself from outside influences, taking no part in the affairs of the world, calming yourself and stilling the mind. As *The Great Cessation and Insight* says, we must 'break all ties with everyday life, human affairs, the arts and scholarship'.

★

When guests are thronging to pay their respects to some highly acclaimed family on a joyous or sorrowful occasion, wandering monks really should not be seen hanging around, mingling with the crowd and ingratiating themselves.

Even if they have some reason for being there, monks should stay aloof from others.

*

I cannot bear the way people will make it their business to know all the details of some current rumour, even though it has nothing to do with them, and then proceed to pass the story on and do their best to learn more. Wandering monks up from some provincial backwater seem particularly adept at prying into tales about others as if it was their own concern, and spreading the word in such detail that you wonder how on earth they came to know so much.

*

People seem to be drawn to pursue precisely those things that are quite unrelated to their normal life.

A monk will practise the arts of the warrior, while uncouth soldiers from the eastern provinces disdain to study archery and instead pretend to know all about the Buddhist Law, or delight in composing linked verse or making music together. Yet they are even more despised for this than for the second-rate performance of their own profession.

Not only monks, but a great many men of even the highest ranks, court nobles and senior courtiers, are fond of the military arts. In fact, however, you may fight a hundred battles and win them all but it still won't assure you fame as a warrior. Anyone can look the part of warrior when luck allows him to overthrow his opponent. It is only when you have run through every weapon, your last arrow is shot, and you accept death without surrendering that you have truly gained such a name. While you still live, you have no cause to boast of your prowess.

The way of the warrior is closer to the behaviour of beasts than of virtuous men; its cultivation is pointless unless you are born of warrior stock.

★

When someone complained that it was a great shame the way fine silk covers are so soon damaged, Ton'a replied, 'It is only after the top and bottom edges of the silk have frayed, or when the mother-of-pearl has peeled off the roller, that a scroll is truly impressive' – an astonishingly fine remark, I felt. Similarly, an unmatched set of bound books can be considered unattractive, but Bishop Kōyū impressed me deeply by saying that only a boring man will always want things to match; real quality lies in irregularity – another excellent remark.

In all things, perfect regularity is tasteless. Something left not quite finished is very appealing, a gesture towards the future. Someone told me that even in the construction of the imperial palace, some part is always left uncompleted.

In the Buddhist scriptures and other works written

by the great men of old there are also a number of missing sections.

*

The Chikurin'in Novice and Minister of the Left was set to advance smoothly to Chief Minister, yet he took the tonsure before promotion, declaring that he would retire while still minister since his future prospects bored him. Later, the Tōin Minister of the Left was very much in sympathy with this; he too was without any ambition to advance to the highest post.

'The dragon that has scaled the heights laments his coming fall,' as the saying goes. The moon swells to the full only to wane; things first prosper and then decay. It is the way of things that whatever has reached its apogee must thereafter decline.

*

No human heart is quite guileless; there is some deceit in all. But why should there not be the occasional person who is honest and upright?

One may not be without guile oneself, but it is human nature to envy others who are wise and good. Really stupid people who come across the rare wise man, however, will hate him. 'He turns up his nose at small gains because in his heart he hopes for bigger ones,' they sneer. 'It's all a hypocritical pose, intended to impress and make a name for himself.'

Such a man scoffs so contemptuously because the other's nature differs from his own, but this only reveals what he himself is like – a born fool, who has no hope of transcending his own nature. Even the pretence of turning down a chance of some small gain would be beyond him; likewise the merest imitation of wisdom.

If you run about the streets pretending to be a madman, then a madman is what you are. If in pretence of being wicked you kill a man, wicked is what you are. A horse that pretends to fleetness must be counted among the fleet; a man who models himself on the saintly Emperor Shun will indeed be among his number. Even a deceitful imitation of wisdom will place you among the wise.

★

The Yin-Yang masters do not concern themselves with those days of the calendar marked 'Red Tongue Days'. Nor did people of old treat the day as unpropitious. It seems someone more recently has declared it unlucky, and now everyone has begun to avoid it, believing that things undertaken on this day will miscarry. This idea – that whatever is said or done on this day will fail, that objects gained on the day will be lost and plans made will go awry – is ridiculous. If you count the number of failures that happen on an auspicious day, you will find there are just as many.

This is because, in this transient phenomenal world with its constant change, what appears to exist in fact does not. What is begun has no end. Aims go unful-filled, yet desire is endless. The human heart changes ceaselessly. All things are passing illusion. What is there that remains unchanging? The folly of such beliefs springs from people's inability to understand this.

It is said that evil performed on an auspicious day is always ill-fated, while good performed on an inauspicious one will be blessed by good fortune. It is people who create good fortune and misfortune, not the calendar.

★

A man who was studying archery took two arrows in his hand and stood before the target.

'A beginner should not hold two arrows,' his teacher told him. 'You will be careless with the first, knowing you have a second. You must always be determined to hit the target with the single arrow you shoot, and have no thought beyond this.' With only two arrows, and standing before his master, would he really be inclined to be slapdash with one of them? Yet although he may not have been aware of his own carelessness, his teacher was. The same injunction surely applies in all matters.

A man engaged in Buddhist practice will tell himself at night that there is always the morning, or in the morning will anticipate the night, always intending to make more effort later. And if such are your days, how much less aware must you be of the passing moment's indolence. Why should it be so difficult to carry something out right now when you think of it, to seize the instant?

*

Someone told the following tale. A man sells an ox. The buyer says he will come in the morning to pay and take the beast. But during the night, the ox dies. 'The buyer thus gained, while the seller lost,' he concluded.

But a bystander remarked, 'The owner did indeed lose on the transaction, but he profited greatly in another way. Let me tell you why. Living creatures have no knowledge of the nearness of death. Such was the ox, and such too are we humans. As it happened, the ox died that night; as it happened, the owner lived on. One day's life is more precious than a fortune's worth of money, while an ox's worth weighs no more than a goose feather. One cannot say that a man who gains a fortune while losing a coin or two has made a loss.'

Everyone laughed at this. 'That reasoning doesn't only apply to the owner of the ox,' they scoffed.

The man went on. 'Well then, if people hate death they should love life. Should we not relish each day the joy of survival? Fools forget this – they go striving after other enjoyments, cease to appreciate the fortune they have and risk all to lay their hands on fresh wealth. Their desires are never sated. There is a deep contradiction in failing to enjoy life and yet fearing death when faced with it. It is because they have no fear of death that people fail to enjoy life – no, not that they don't fear it, but rather they forget its nearness. Of course, it must be said that the ultimate gain lies in transcending the relative world with its distinction between life and death.'

At this, everyone jeered more than ever.

*

There are endless examples of something that attaches itself to another, eats away at it and harms it. A body has fleas. A house has rats. A nation has robbers. A lesser man has wealth. An honourable man has moral imperatives. A monk has the Buddhist Law.

*

Here are some things that particularly spoke to me among the teachings I read in a book called *Superb Small Sermons* or something of the sort, a collection of the teachings of venerable holy men:

– When hesitating between doing and not doing something, it is generally better not to do it.

– One with his thoughts fixed on the world to come should not own so much as a pickling jar. Even the possession of a fine copy of the sutras or a nicely made Buddhist image is wrong.

– The highest way of living for those who take the tonsure is to aim to lack nothing while owning nothing.

– Monks of high degree should become as lowly monks, a wise man should become foolish, a wealthy man poor, a skilled man talentless.

– If you wish to follow the Buddhist Way, you should simply retire and make time in your life, and not let your mind dwell on worldly matters. This is the most important thing.

I have forgotten the others.

★

No one begrudges the passing moment. Is this because they are wise, or because they are fools? To the lazy fools among them I would say: a single coin may be next to worthless, but it is through their accumulation that the poor man becomes rich. This is why the merchant is so keen to save every coin he can. You may not be aware of the moments, but as long as they continue to pass, you will very soon find yourself at the end of life. Thus, one dedicated to the Way must not concern himself over the distant future. His only care should be not to let the present moment slip vainly through his fingers.

Imagine someone comes to you and announces that you will die tomorrow. How will you spend your last day? What entertainment could you find? How would you busy yourself? And how is this day we are now living different from that final day?

We inevitably waste most of each day in eating and drinking, defecating, sleeping, talking and walking about. For the tiny remainder of our time, we do worthless things, speak worthless words, think worthless thoughts. And not only do we pass the moments in this way, but whole days, whole months pass thus – a lifetime. This is supreme folly.

Xie Lingyun was recorder of the translation of *The Lotus Sutra*, but he was taken up with thoughts of his own advancement, so Hui Yuan refused to include him in his pious Bailian group.

Lose for a moment your grasp of the passing instant and you are as good as dead. You ask why time should be so precious? It is so that you may concentrate the mind on banishing all idle thoughts, refrain from engaging in worldly matters and meditate if this is what you choose, or perform austerities if that is your chosen path.

*

I once asked someone skilled at the board game of *sugoroku* for hints on how to play. 'Don't play to win,' he said. 'Play not to lose. Consider what moves would make you lose most quickly, and avoid them. Choose a method that will make you lose after your opponent, even if only by a single square.'

This lesson from one who knows his art equally applies to the arts of governing both self and nation.

*

No one, hearing that someone is setting out the next day on a long journey, will confront them with something to attend to that requires their calm and undivided attention. A man in the midst of a sudden major upheaval or terrible sorrow is in no position to listen to talk about other matters, or to enquire about the griefs and joys of others. No one would think to complain of his remissness. And the same applies, surely, to those of advancing years or visited by illness, not to mention those who have chosen to leave the world for a life of religious devotion.

None of the requirements of human interaction and etiquette can be easily avoided. If we insist on being punctilious in all those worldly demands so difficult to ignore, it will only add to desires, shackle our lives and leave no space in our hearts for calm detachment, and we will end up wasting our entire life being driven to distraction by trivial matters.

'Night closes in, the way is long. / My feet have stumbled on life's road.' Now is the time to cast off all worldly ties. Turn your back on loyalty. Think no more of propriety. Those who fail to understand are free to call you mad, deranged, lacking all feeling. No censure can hurt you now, nor praise sway you.

*

A large group of *boro* priests had gathered at a place called Shukugahara and were chanting the Nine Nenbutsus, when another from elsewhere arrived, and asked if there was a monk by the name of Irowoshi among them.

'I am Irowoshi,' came a voice from their midst. 'Who speaks?'

'My name is Shirabonji. I've heard that my teacher' – he gave a name – 'was killed by a *boro* named Irowoshi up in the eastern provinces. I ask because I'm hoping to meet this man and repay the grudge I owe him.'

'Bravely spoken! It happened as you describe. If we face off here, we will desecrate holy ground. Let's fight it out on the riverbank over there. Please don't come to the aid of either of us, my friends. If too many people get caught up in this it will interfere with the rituals.'

Having agreed on this, the two went off to the riverbank and fell to, slashing at each other for all they were worth, till both were dead.

I think *boro* may be a recent phenomenon. These days, it is said that their origins were variously called *boronji*, *bonji* or *kanji*. They are like renunciates in appearance, but in fact they are deeply attached to the ego; they appear to yearn for the Buddhist Way, yet they specialize in fighting.

To all appearances these *boro* are shameless and high-handed ruffians, but the complete disregard for death revealed by this story strikes me as impressive, so I decided to set it down as it was told to me.

*

The domestic animals are the horse and the ox. It is a shame to tether the poor things and make them suffer, but it can't be helped, since they are indispensable to us. One should most certainly have a dog, as they are better than men at guarding the house. However, since all the houses around you will have dogs, you probably don't need to go out of your way to get one yourself.

All other creatures, be it bird or beast, are useless. When you lock an animal that runs free into a cage or chain it up, when you snip the wings of a flying bird and confine it, the beast will ceaselessly pine for the wild and the bird for the clouds. Surely no one with a heart to imagine how unbearable he himself would find it could take pleasure in these creatures' torment. It would take the stony heart of a Jie or a Zhou to enjoy witnessing the suffering of a living creature.

Wang Huizhi loved birds. He watched them frolicking happily in the forest, and made them his companions in his rambles. He did not catch them and make them suffer. We should follow the words of the classic: 'Do not cultivate rare birds or strange beasts in your own land.'

★

Anyone who wastes time in worthless pursuits must be called a fool or a villain. Obligation compels us to do many things for the sake of lord and nation, and we have little enough time left for ourselves. Think of it like this: we have an inescapable need, first, to acquire food, second, clothes, and third, a place to live. These and these alone are the three great necessities of human life. To live without hunger or cold, sheltered from the elements and at peace – this is happiness.

Yet we are all prey to sickness, and once ill the

wretchedness of it is hard to bear, so we should add medical treatment to our list. Thus, we have four things without which a man is poor, while a man who lacks none of these is rich. It is sheer self-indulgence to pursue anything beyond these four. With these four in moderation, no one could be said to lack anything in life.

*

The monk Zehō is among the finest scholars in the Pure Land sect, yet he doesn't parade his learning; he lives in calm seclusion, chanting the *nenbutsu* day in day out. An exemplary existence.

*

Grand Counsellor Masafusa was a fine, scholarly man, and the retired emperor was planning to promote him to Commander of the Guards, when someone in close service informed His Majesty that he had just witnessed something dreadful.

'What was it?' His Majesty enquired.

'I watched through a gap in the fence as Count Masafusa cut off the leg of a live dog to feed to his hawk,' the man replied.

His Majesty was appalled. The thought of Masafusa revolted him, and he was not promoted after all.

It is extraordinary that such a man would own a hawk, and the story of the dog's leg is absolutely unfounded. The lie was most unfortunate, but how splendid of His

Majesty to have reacted with such disgust when he heard the tale.

Overall, it must be said that those who kill or harm living creatures, or set them up to fight each other for their own pleasure, are no better than wild beasts themselves. If you pause and look carefully at the birds and animals, and even the little insects, you will see that they love their children, feel affection for their parents, live in couples, are jealous, angry, full of desire, self-protecting and fearful for their lives, and far more so than men, since they lack all intelligence. Surely one should pity them when they are killed or made to suffer? If you can look on any sentient being without compassion, you are less than human.

★

Yan Hui's firm belief was that he must avoid burdening others. One should not cause suffering and pain to others, nor undermine the will of the humble man.

Some will take pleasure in deceiving, frightening or mocking little children. Adults treat such tales lightly, knowing that they are quite unfounded, but those words will strike deep into the heart of a poor little child, and humiliate, terrify or appal it. It is heartless to enjoy tormenting children in this way.

The joys, angers, sorrows and pleasures of adults too are all based on illusion, but who among us is not attached to the seeming reality of this life?

It harms a man more to wound his heart than to hurt

his body. Illness, too, often originates in the mind. Few illnesses come from without. There are times when medicine cannot produce the intended sweat, but shame or fear will always bring one on, which should prove to us that such things come from the mind. We find examples in the classics, after all – think of the man who was hoisted up the Ling Yun Tower to write its signboard, whose hair turned white from fear at the height.

*

It is best to keep the peace with others, bend your own will to conform with theirs and put yourself last and others first.

Those who enjoy the competition of games of every kind do so because they love to win. They delight in their own superior skill. Clearly, then, the loser must feel equivalently downcast. Nor does one derive any enjoyment from choosing to lose in order to please one's competitor. It is unethical to give yourself pleasure by depriving others of it.

When relaxing with close friends, too, some enjoy proving their own wit superior by setting others up and deceiving them. This is most discourteous. Such behaviour has led to much long-standing bitterness, begun innocently enough at a social gathering. All these evils spring from a love of contest.

If you wish to be better than others, you should aim to excel them through study; by pursuing truth, you will learn not to take pride in your virtues or compete with others. It takes the strength conferred by study to enable you to relinquish high office and to turn your back on gain.

★

A certain *samādhi* monk of the Lotus Hall at Retired Emperor Takakura's tomb one day picked up a mirror and took a good look at his face. The shocking ugliness of his own visage filled him with such despair that he found the very mirror repulsive; for a long time afterwards he continued to fear mirrors so much that he wouldn't even touch one, and he avoided the society of others. He secluded himself away, only emerging to take part in the temple's devotions. I was very struck to hear this story.

Even people who seem eminently intelligent will judge others yet have no knowledge of themselves. It makes no sense to lack self-knowledge while understanding those around you. He who knows himself must be said to be the man of real knowledge.

We do not realize that we are ugly, that we are fools, that we are inexpert in our field, worthless, old, a prey to illness, that death is just around the corner, that our Buddhist practice is inadequate. We know nothing of our own faults, let alone of others' criticism of us. Yet we can see ourselves in the mirror. We can count up our years. We do know something of ourselves, yet because we are helpless to change things we could essentially be said to know nothing.

I am not suggesting that we should change our face

or make ourselves young again. But why not simply abandon something if you realize your lack of skill? Why not retire to some quiet place and live at ease once you discover you are old? And why, when a man understands that his practice is inadequate, would he not search his soul on the matter?

It is always shameful to mix with those who don't welcome you. A man with an ugly face and poor intelligence will nevertheless go into service, an ignorant man will mingle with the erudite, a talentless fellow will join in with highly skilled practitioners, a white-haired old codger will fraternize with men in their prime; people yearn for the unattainable, bewail matters beyond their power, wait for things that will never come, fear others or fawn on them. The shame in all this is not caused by others. You bring it on yourself by your own greed. This insatiable desire is due to a lack of real understanding that the end of life, that tremendous thing, is at this very moment as good as upon us.

*

Should we look at the spring blossoms only in full flower, or the moon only when cloudless and clear? To long for the moon with the rain before you, or to lie curtained in your room while the spring passes unseen, is yet more poignant and deeply moving. A branch of blossoms on the verge of opening, a garden strewn with fading petals, have more to please the eye. Could poems on the themes of 'Going to view the blossoms to find them already fallen' or 'Written when I was prevented from going to see the flowers' be deemed inferior to 'On seeing the blossoms'? It is natural human feeling to yearn over the falling blossoms and the setting moon – yet some, it seems, are so insensitive that they will declare that since this branch and that have already shed their flowers, there is nothing worth seeing any longer.

In all things, the beginning and end are the most engaging. Does the love of man and woman suggest only their embraces? No, the sorrow of lovers parted before they met, laments over promises betrayed, long lonely nights spent sleepless until dawn, pining thoughts for one in some far place, a woman left sighing over past love in her tumbledown abode – it is these, surely, that embody the romance of love.

Rather than gazing on a clear full moon that shines over a thousand leagues, it is infinitely more moving to see the moon near dawn and after long anticipation, tinged with most beautiful palest blue, a moon glimpsed among cedar branches deep in the mountains, its light now hidden again by the gathering clouds of an autumn shower. The moist glint of moonlight on the glossy leaves of the forest *shii* oak or the white oak pierces the heart, and makes you yearn for the distant capital and a friend of true sensibility to share the moment with you.

Are blossoms and the moon merely things to be gazed at with the eye? No, it brings more contentment and delight to stay inside the house in spring and, there in your bedroom, let your heart go out to the unseen moonlit night.

The man of quality never appears entranced by anything; he savours things with a casual air. Country bumpkins, however, take flamboyant pleasure in everything. They will wriggle their way in through the crowd and stand there endlessly gaping up at the blossoms, sit about under the trees drinking sake and indulging in linked verse-making together and, finally, oafishly break off great branches of blossom to carry away. They will dip their hands and feet into clear spring water, get down to stand in unsullied snow and leave their footprints everywhere, and in short throw themselves into everything with uninhibited glee.

I have observed such people behaving quite astonishingly when they came to see the Kamo festival. Declaring that the procession was horribly late so there was no point in hanging around on the viewing stand, a group retired to a house behind the stands and settled down to eat, drink and play *go* and *sugoroku*, leaving one of their number back on the stand to keep watch. 'It's coming by!' he shouted, whereupon they all leaped frantically to their feet and dashed back, elbowing each other out of the way as they scrambled up, nearly tumbling off in their eagerness to thrust aside the blinds for a better look, jostling for position and craning to miss nothing, and commenting volubly on everything they saw. Then, when that section of the procession had passed, off they went again, declaring they'd be back for the next one. They were clearly only there to see the spectacle.

The upper echelons from the capital, on the other

hand, will sit there dozing without so much as a glance at the scene. Young gentlemen of lesser rank are constantly rising to wait on their superiors, while those seated in the back rows never rudely lean forward, and no one goes out of his way to watch as the procession passes.

On the day of the festival everything is elegantly strewn with the emblematic *aoi* leaves, and even before dawn the carriages quietly begin to arrive to secure a good viewing position, everyone intrigued about which carriage is whose, sometimes identifying them by an accompanying servant or ox-boy they recognize. It is endlessly fascinating to watch the carriages come and go, some charming, others more showy. By the time evening draws in, all those rows of carriages and the people who were crammed into the stands have disappeared, and hardly a soul is left. Once the chaos of departing carriages is over, the blinds and matting are taken down from the stands as you watch, and the place is left bare and forlorn, moving you to a poignant sense of the brevity of worldly things. It is this that is the real point of seeing the festival.

Among the people coming and going in front of the stands there are many you recognize, making you realize there are not really so many people in this world. Even if you were destined to die after all these others, clearly your own death cannot be far away. When a large vessel filled with water is pierced with a tiny hole, though each drop is small it will go on relentlessly leaking until soon the vessel is empty. The city is filled with people, but not a day would go by without someone dying. And is it only one or two a day? There are times when the corpses on the pyres of Toribe, Funaoka and elsewhere further afield are piled high, but no day passes without a funeral. And so the coffin sellers no sooner make one than it is sold. Be they young, be they strong, the time of death comes upon all unawares. It is an extraordinary miracle that we have escaped it until now. Can we ever, even briefly, have peace of mind in this world?

It is like the game of *mamakodate*, played with *sugoroku* pieces, in which no one knows which in the line of pieces will be removed next – when the count is made and a piece is taken, the rest seem to have escaped, but the count goes on and more are picked off in turn, so that no piece is finally spared. Soldiers going into battle, aware of the closeness of death, forget their home and their own safety. And it is sheer folly for a man who lives secluded from the world in his lowly hut, spending his days in idle delight in his garden, to pass off such matters as irrelevant to himself. Do you imagine that the enemy Impermanence will not come forcing its way into your peaceful mountain retreat? The recluse faces death as surely as the soldier setting forth to battle.

*

The trees one wants in a garden are the pine and the cherry. Of the pines, the white pine is good. As for blossoms, the single cherry is best. The double cherry was once found only in the old capital of Nara, but these days it is everywhere, it seems. The cherries of Yoshino and the Left Guard cherry are all single flowers. The double cherry is a peculiar thing, gaudy and distorted, and there is no need to have it in the garden. The late-flowering cherry is also unattractive. It is repulsive to see it crawling with insects.

As for blossoming plums, the white and the pale crimson are best. The single one that flowers early, the double crimson with its lovely smell – all are delightful. The late plum that flowers with the cherry is not so interesting. The cherry blossom overwhelms it, and the sight of the withered blooms on its boughs is also mournful. The Kyōgoku Counsellor Novice planted single-flowering plums close to his eaves, because he was charmed by the impetuous way they flower and scatter before all the other blossom trees. Two of the trees apparently still stand on the south side of his Kyōgoku residence.

Willows are also delightful. The young maple leaves of the fourth month are more beautiful than any flowers or autumn leaves. Both *tachibana* and *katsura* trees should be old and large.

As for plants: the kerria, the wisteria, the iris and the carnation pink. For ponds: the lotus. Plants for autumn: miscanthus reeds, plume grass, the bellflower, the bush clover, yellow valerian, the *fujibakama*, the aster, the burnet, the themeda, the gentian, the white chrysanthemum. Also the yellow chrysanthemum. The ivy, kudzu vine and morning glory should trail over low fences and not be left to grow too high or thick.

It is very hard to feel fond of other plants – rare ones,

or those with off-putting Chinesey names or unfamiliar flowers. Generally speaking, the rare and strange are things that please the lower type. It is best not to have them.

*

A sensible man will not die leaving valuables behind. A collection of vulgar objects looks bad, while good ones will suggest a futile attachment to worldly things. And it is even more unfortunate to leave behind a vast accumulation. There will be ugly fights over it after your death, with everyone determined to get things for himself. If you plan to leave something to a particular person, you should pass it on while you are still alive.

Some things are necessary for day-to-day living, but one should have nothing else.

*

Even people who seem to lack any finer feelings will sometimes say something impressive.

An alarming-looking ruffian from the eastern provinces once turned to the man beside him and asked if he had any children. 'Not one,' the man replied.

'Well then,' said the Easterner, 'you'll not know what true depth of feeling is. It frightens me to think of a man unacquainted with tenderness. It's having your own children that brings home to you the poignant beauty of life.'

This is indeed true. Without familial love, would

such a man as this be able to feel compassion? Even a man who lacks all filial piety will discover how a parent feels when he himself has children.

It is wrong for a man who has taken the tonsure and cast all away to despise those he sees around him encumbered with worldly ties, who go crawling abjectly after this person and that and are full of craving. If you imagined yourself in his place, you would see how he might abase himself so far as to steal for the sake of his beloved parents or wife and children. Rather than seizing thieves and punishing their crimes, it would be better to make the world a place where people did not go hungry or cold. A man without stable means is a man whose heart is unstable. People steal from extremity. There will be no end to crime while the world is not governed well, and men suffer from cold and starvation. It is cruel to make people suffer and drive them to break the law, then treat the poor creatures as criminals.

As for how to improve people's lives, there can be no doubt that it would benefit those below if people in high positions were to cease their luxurious and wasteful ways and instead were kind and tender to the people, and encouraged agriculture. The true criminal must be defined as a man who commits a crime though he is as decently fed and clothed as others.

*

When someone reports that a man has died a fine death, one would be impressed enough with the modest statement that he died peacefully and without distress – but fools will go on to add details about the man's strange or unusual appearance at the time, or elaborately praise his deathbed words or gestures to suit their own fancy, making you doubt that this is the same man as he would have been in life.

Even an avatar of the Buddha himself is in no position to pronounce on this great event, nor can the wisest scholar gauge it. Enough that the man himself dies without error – a death should not be judged by what others may have witnessed.

★

Somebody has remarked that if you have not become adept at an art by the time you are fifty, you should give up. You do not have the time left to make further efforts worthwhile.

People should not laugh at the old. It is painful and off-putting to see old men mixing with society. As a rule, those over fifty are most seemly when they withdraw from all activities and retire to a leisured life, and this is what they ought to do. A man is a fool if he spends his entire life involved with worldly affairs. If there is something you wish to know, by all means ask instruction of others, but once you have grasped the facts well enough to feel clear about the question, pursue it no further. The ideal is not to desire to know in the first place.

If you would take the world on its own terms, you need above all to read the mood of the moment. If the timing isn't right, your words will grate on your listeners and upset them, and your plans will come to nothing. You must know how to recognize such occasions.

There is no choosing your moment, however, when it comes to illness, childbirth or death. You cannot call these things off because 'the time isn't right'. The truly momentous events of life – the changes from birth through life, transformation and death – are like the powerful current of a raging river. They surge ever forward without a moment's pause. Thus, when it comes to the essentials, both in religious and in worldly life, you should not wait for the right moment in what you wish to achieve, nor dawdle over preparations. Your feet must never pause.

Summer does not come once spring is done, nor autumn arrive at the end of summer. Spring begins early to hold summer's intimations, while hints of autumn already come and go within summer, and no sooner is autumn here than winter's cold begins. The tenth month, winter's start, has a spring-like warmth that greens the plants and swells the buds on the plum. The leaves of trees, too, do not fall before the new shoots begin. They fall unable to withstand the pressure from beneath, where the young leaves are already forming. The tree is prepared and waiting from within, and so each change presses swiftly forward.

Still swifter are the changes through human life, from birth to old age, sickness and death. The seasons progress in a fixed order. Not so the time of death. We do not always see its approach; it can come upon us from behind. People know that they will die, but death will surprise them while they believe it is not yet close. It is as if we gaze at the far-off ebb-tide flats while even now the sea is rising to flood the rocks we stand on.

*

To take up the brush is to write, to take up an instrument is to feel the urge to make it sing. A sake cup in the hand provokes the thought of sake, while a dice in your palm will prompt ideas of gambling. Contact will always trigger the associated urge. Never for a moment indulge in wrongful pastimes.

A passing glance at a phrase from the holy teachings will lead the eye on to read the words surrounding it, and before you know it you may have righted years of error. Had you not opened the text just then, you might never have had that realization. This is an example of the virtue of contact. Even if you lack all faith, simply to seat yourself before an image, hold a rosary and take up a sutra book is to perform a virtuous act, however perfunctory; even seated on your meditation chair with distracted mind, you will sink into meditation before you know it.

Phenomena and their essence are intrinsically one. If outward actions conform, inner realization will naturally follow. Do not decry a lack of faith – such 'empty gestures' in fact deserve our reverence.

★

The way people struggle to get along in the world strikes me as like fashioning a buddha from snow on a spring day, decking it out with precious metals and jewels, then setting out to build a worship hall for it. Would it survive long enough to be placed in the finished hall?

So many strive in hopes of the future, even as the life still in them is daily dissolving away like snow from beneath the snowman.

★

It is not good to call on someone if you have no particular reason. Even if you go with some purpose, you should leave promptly once your business is accomplished. It is very annoying if a visit drags on.

There is so much talking when people get together. It is exhausting, disturbs the peace of mind and wastes time better spent on other things. There is nothing to be gained for either party. It is bad, too, to feel irritable as you talk. When you don't care for something, you should come right out and say so.

The exception to all this is when someone after your own heart, whom you feel inclined to talk with, is at a loose end and encourages you to stay a while longer for a peaceful chat. No doubt we all have Ruan Ji's 'welcoming green eyes' from time to time.

It is very nice when a friend simply drops in, has a quiet talk with you, and then leaves. It is also wonderfully pleasing to receive a letter that simply begins, 'I write because it's been some time since I sent news,' or some such.

★

A young man overflows with vigour, things stir his heart, and he is prone to passions. Like a flung ball, such a youth courts danger and physical harm. Riches are wasted in pursuit of magnificence, then all this is suddenly abandoned for the wretched robes of the monk; he is full of fervour and fight, suffers agonies of shame or bitterness, and his fancies are constantly shifting from day to day. He will devote himself to women and pursue infatuations, or take his example from those who have died with no thought to their own safety or longevity, behaving with such reckless daring that 'a long life lies ruined', or let himself be drawn wherever his heart urges, becoming the cause of talk for many years to come. It is indeed in youth that we make our mistakes.

In age, on the other hand, the spirit weakens, we become indifferent and apathetic, and nothing rouses us. The heart grows naturally calm, so that we no longer act in futile ways but instead tend to our bodies, live free of discontent and try to avoid troubling others.

Age has more wisdom than youth, just as youth has more beauty than does age.

★

It is said that a dog used for hunting with small hawks will be spoiled for this sport if used with large hawks. This holds a universal truth – follow the great, and you will abandon the small.

Among all the many things in life, nothing is more fulfilling than delighting in the Way. This is indeed the truly great thing. What can you not relinquish when once you have heard of and committed yourself to the Way of Buddhism? To what else could you devote your energies? Even a fool is surely wiser than a clever dog.

★

There are many incomprehensible things in this world.

I cannot understand why people will seize any occasion to immediately bring out the sake, delighting in forcing someone else to drink. The other will frown and grimace in painful protest, attempt to throw it away when no one's looking or do his best to escape, but this man will seize him, pin him down and make him swallow cup after cup. A genteel man will quickly be transformed into a madman and start acting the fool; a vigorous, healthy fellow will before your very eyes become shockingly afflicted and fall senseless to the floor. What a thing to do, on a day of celebration! Right into the next day his head hurts, he can't eat, and he lies there groaning with all memory of the previous day gone as if it were a former life. He neglects essential duties both public and private, with disastrous effects. It is both boorish and cruel to subject someone to this sort of misery. Surely a man who has had this bitter experience will be filled with regret and loathing. Anyone from a land that lacked this custom would be amazed and appalled to hear of its existence in another country.

It is depressing enough just to witness this happening to another. A man who had always seemed thoughtful and refined will burst into mindless laughter, prattle on and on, his lacquered court cap askew, the ties of his robes loosened and the skirts hauled up above his shins, and generally behave so obliviously that he seems a changed man. A woman will blatantly push her hair up away from her face, throw back her head and laugh quite shamelessly, and seize the hand of the person with the sake, while the more uncouth might grab one of the snacks and hold it to someone else's mouth or eat it herself – a quite disgraceful sight. People bellow at the top of their lungs, everyone sings and prances about, and an old monk is called in, who proceeds to bare his filthy black shoulder and writhe about so that you can hardly stand to watch, and you loathe just as much the others who sit there enjoying the spectacle.

Some will make you cringe by the way they sing their own praises, others will cry into their drink, while the lower orders abuse each other and get into quite shocking and appalling fights. Finally, after all manner of disgraceful and pitiful behaviour, the drunkard will seize things without permission, then end up hurting himself by rolling off the veranda or tumbling from his horse or carriage. If he's of a class that goes on foot he'll stagger away down the high road, doing unspeakable things against people's walls or gates as he goes. It is quite disgusting to see the old monk in his black robe stumbling off, steadying himself with his hand on the shoulder of the lad beside him and rambling on incomprehensibly.

If drinking like this profited us in this world or the next, what could one say? But in this world it leads to all manner of error, and causes both illness and loss of wealth. Wine has been called 'the greatest of medicines', but in fact all sickness springs from it. It is claimed that you forget your sorrows in drink, but from what I can see, men in their cups will in fact weep to recall their past unhappiness. As for the next world – having lost the wisdom you were born with, reduced all your good karma to ashes, built up a store of wickedness and broken all the Buddhist precepts, you are destined for hell. Remember, the Buddha teaches that those who lift the wine glass either to their own lips or to others' will spend five hundred lifetimes without hands.

Yet, loathsome though one finds it, there are situations when a cup of sake is hard to resist. On a moonlit night, a snowy morning, or beneath the flowering cherry trees, it increases all the pleasures of the moment to bring out the sake cups and settle down to talk serenely together over a drink. It is also a great comfort to have a drink together if an unexpected friend calls round when time is hanging heavy on your hands. And it is quite wonderful when sake and snacks are elegantly served from behind her curtains by some remote and exalted lady.

It is also quite delightful to sit across from a close friend in some cosy little nook in winter, roasting food over the coals and drinking lots of sake together. And delightful too on a journey to sit about on the grass together in some wayside hut or out in the wild, drinking and lamenting the lack of a suitable snack. And it's a fine thing when someone who really hates having sake pressed on them is forced to have just a little. You are thrilled when some grand person singles you out and offers to refill your cup, urging, 'Do have more. You've barely drunk.' And it is also very pleasing when someone you would like to get to know better is a drinker and becomes very pally with you in his cups.

All things considered, a drunkard is so entertaining he can be forgiven his sins. Think of the charming scene when a master throws open the door on his servant, who is sound asleep next morning after an exhausting night on the drink. The poor befuddled fellow rushes off, rubbing his bleary eyes, topknot exposed on his hatless head, only half dressed and clutching the rest of his trailing clothes, his hairy shins sticking out below his lifted skirts as he scampers into the distance – a typical drunk.

A man decided to make his son a monk. 'Study the laws of karmic cause and effect,' he told him, 'and make your living by preaching.'

The lad did as instructed. First, in order to be a successful preacher, he learned how to ride a horse – he had no palanquin or carriage, after all, and it seemed to him that, if his services were called for and a horse were sent to fetch him, it would be a sorry business if he had a bad riding seat and fell off. Next, he learned some popular songs, for a monk can be regaled with sake after the service is over, and the client would be very unimpressed if he couldn't entertain the gathering in some way. When he had finally gained some competence in these two skills he felt the urge to improve them further, and in the end he grew old having devoted all his time to them with none to spare for learning how to actually preach.

He is not the only one; all of us have this experience. While we are young, we have all manner of ambitious plans for the future – to make a success of ourselves in life, achieve grand things, learn skills, study. But there seems plenty of time to fulfil our wishes, and we dawdle on the way, letting ourselves be distracted by the passing concerns of everyday life, so that we grow old having in fact done nothing much. Regret them as we might, there is no regaining our lost years, and, like a wheel running ever faster downhill, debility overtakes us, while we have succeeded in learning no skill and never achieved the success we dreamed of in life.

Thus, you should carefully consider which among the main things you want in life is the most important, and renounce all the others to dedicate yourself to that thing alone. Among the many matters that press in on us on any day, at any given moment, we must give ourselves to the most productive, by no matter how little – ignore the rest, and devote yourself entirely to the most important thing. If you find yourself reluctant to abandon the others, you will never achieve your primary aim.

It is like a *go* player who never wastes a move, but gets the better of his opponent by sacrificing the small in favour of the large. Here, it is easy to sacrifice three stones to gain ten, but not so easy if you must lose ten to gain eleven. He should always pursue a course that gains him more, even if it is a single extra stone, but when the profit is so marginal a player is often loath to sacrifice the ten precious stones he has accumulated. The urge to cling to one thing while grasping for another will cause the loss of both.

If a man in the capital has urgent business in the eastern hills, but once he arrives at the door realizes that he would gain more by going to the western hills, he should turn around then and there and go west. 'Now that I'm here, I may as well finish my business in the east,' he may think. 'After all, no day was fixed for that other matter. I'll make a decision about it once I'm home.' But the moment's lazy impulse will lead to a lifetime's negligence. You must be very wary of this.

Once you are committed to achieving your one aim,

there is no use grieving over the failure of the others. Nor should you be ashamed to be mocked by others. Unless you forgo the many, you will not attain that one great thing.

Here is a strange and marvellous tale: someone at a gathering mentioned that there were varying names for types of plume grass, such as *masaho* and *masoho*, and added that the holy man of Watanabe knew the poetic teachings on this matter. The monk Tōren was among those who heard this.

It was raining at the time. 'Can someone lend me a raincoat and rain hat?' he said. 'I'm off to find this holy man and learn the details of this matter from him.'

'No need to be so hasty,' people said. 'Wait till the rain's over.'

'Don't be ridiculous,' replied Tōren. 'Does a man's life wait for a break in the weather? I may die, the holy man may die, and then there would be no chance to ask.' Whereupon he hurried off, and the story goes that he received his answer.

'Swiftness will always bear fruit,' as the work known as the *Analects* says. We should seize the moment to turn our thoughts to that one great matter of the Buddhist Truth with the same alacrity with which Tōren pursued his urge to learn about the plume grass.

*

You can decide to do something today, but before you manage it some unexpected and urgent business will arise to overwhelm your plan for the day, or the person you are waiting for is unable to come, or someone unexpected arrives, or something you were relying on turns out differently, so that the only things that go well are things you hadn't anticipated. Matters that threatened to be difficult prove easy, while those that should be straightforward turn out to cause you great pains. The progress of each passing day is quite unlike your anticipation of it. And the same goes for a year – and for a life.

Yet if you assume that everything you anticipate will go awry, you find that in fact some things don't, which makes it all the more difficult to plan. The only certain truth to learn is that all is uncertain.

*

An ignorant person will always be wrong when he sizes up another and believes he can judge the other's intelligence.

It is a grave mistake for a foolish fellow who has to his credit the single fact that he is very good at the art of *go*, to decide that an intelligent man who happens to have no skill at *go* is therefore his intellectual inferior, or for someone skilled in any of the crafts to think himself superior because others do not understand his speciality. Scholar priests who know nothing of meditation, and meditation monks who eschew scholarship, are both wrong to judge each other as inferior.

One should never feel rivalry towards those in other fields, or pass judgement on them.

★

When the now-deceased Tokudaiji Minister of the Right was Superintendent of Police, he was one day holding court at his central gate when the ox of one of the officers, Akikane, broke loose, got into the court room, scrambled up on to the Superintendent's seating platform and there settled down to chew its cud. This was deemed a disturbingly untoward event, and everyone present declared that the beast should be taken off for Yin-Yang divination to determine the meaning.

However, when the Superintendent's father the Minister heard of this, he declared, 'An ox has no understanding. It has its four legs which can take it anywhere. There is no reason to impound a skinny beast that happens to have brought some lowly official here.' He had the ox returned to its master, and changed the matting where the ox had lain. There were no ill consequences from the event.

It is sometimes said that if you see something sinister and choose to treat it as normal, you will thereby avert whatever it portended.

★

Nothing in this world can be trusted. Fools put all their faith in things, and so become angry and bitter.

The powerful should place no faith in their powerful position. The strong are the first to go. The rich should never depend on their wealth. A fortune can easily disappear from one moment to the next. A scholar should never be complacent about his skills. Even Confucius did not meet with the reception he deserved. The virtuous should not rely on their virtue. Even the exemplary Yan Hui met with misfortune. Nor should those favoured by the emperor be smug. You may at any time find yourself instead faced with execution for some crime. Never rely on your servants to be loyal. They can rebel and flee. Never put your faith in others' goodwill. They will inevitably change their minds. Never depend on a promise made. People seldom keep their word.

If you rely neither on yourself nor on others, you will rejoice when things go well, and not be aggrieved when they don't. Maintain a clear space on either side, and nothing will obstruct you; keep open before and behind you, and you will be unimpeded. If you let yourself be hemmed in, you can be squeezed to breaking point. Without care and flexibility in your dealings with the world, you will find yourself in conflict and be damaged, while if you live calmly and serenely, not a hair on your head will come to harm.

Humans are the most miraculous and exalted of all things in heaven and earth. And heaven and earth are boundless. How, then, could we differ in essence? If our spirit is open and boundless, neither fear nor joy will obstruct it, and we will remain untroubled by the world.

Here is what a very rich man once said to me:

'People should put all other things aside and devote themselves single-mindedly to acquiring wealth. There is no point in living if you're poor. Only the rich are worthy of the name "human".

'To gain wealth, you should first cultivate the right spirit. And what spirit might that be? Why, the firm belief that the human world is immutable, and never so much as a moment's pause to consider impermanence. This is the most important thing.

'Next, you must not attend to life's various demands. In this world of ours, there is no end to our own and others' wants. If you follow your desires in what you set out to attain, all your money will be gone before you know it, no matter how much you may have. Desire is limitless, while money is finite. You cannot use limited resources to fulfil unlimited craving. You must be immensely wary of indulging even the smallest urge, and treat any desire that might rear its head as a wicked impulse that is bound to ruin you.

'Next, be aware that if you treat your money like a mere servant, you will very soon find yourself in dire straits. You must venerate it like a revered master, worship it like a god and never bend it to your will. Next, avoid anger and bitterness if you meet with embarrassments in life. Next, always be honest, and honour all promises. For those who follow these rules in seeking wealth, riches will come as inevitably as fire catches dried wood or water flows downhill. Once you have stock-piled unlimited wealth, your desires – for banqueting, music, beautiful women, a finely appointed house – may go unmet, but you will always feel fulfilled and at peace,' he said.

People do indeed seek wealth in order to fulfil their desires. Money is seen as riches because it allows one to gain what one covets. Someone who has desire but does not fulfil it, who has money but does not use it, is essentially no different from a poor man. What might such a person find pleasure in? This man's teaching can be seen as an admonishment to relinquish worldly desires and not lament poverty. Far better, surely, not to have wealth than to find your pleasure in attaining your desires. Far better to avoid contracting boils and pustules in the first place than to find your pleasure in bathing them.

Once you have attained this state, there is no distinction between wealth and poverty. Enlightenment and delusion are one in Buddhist teaching. Great desire and desirelessness have much in common.

★

People do not simply take it into their heads to walk into some house if the owner is present. But if a house is empty, passers-by will casually come in, the lack of human presence will encourage foxes and owls to make themselves at home there, and tree spirits and suchlike bizarre creatures will even appear.

Likewise, since a mirror has no inherent shape or colour, everything can appear reflected in it. If it had its own colour and shape, it wouldn't reflect other things.

The emptiness of space allows it to contain things. The fact that thoughts can come crowding into our mind at will must mean that 'mind' is actually an empty space too. If someone were really in residence there, it would surely not be invaded by all these thoughts.

*

There is a place in Tamba called Izumo, where the deity of the great Izumo Shrine has been installed in a magnificent shrine building. The area is ruled by a certain Shida, who one autumn invited a great many people, including the holy man Shōkai. 'Come and pray to Izumo,' he said, 'and let us feast on rice cakes.' He led them to the shrine, and every one of them prayed and was filled with faith.

The holy man was immensely moved by the sight of the guardian Chinese lion and Korean dog, which were placed back to back and facing backwards. 'How marvellous!' he exclaimed, close to tears. 'Such an unusual position to stand them in! There must be some deep reason behind it.' Then he turned to the others. 'How can you not have noticed this wonder?' he cried. 'I'm amazed at you.'

They were very struck. 'Yes indeed,' they all declared, 'they *are* different from elsewhere. We'll tell this to everyone back in the capital.'

The holy man now wished to learn more, so he called over an elderly and wise-looking shrine priest. 'There must be some interesting tale explaining the placement of these images,' he said. 'Do be so kind as to tell us.'

'Indeed there is,' replied the priest. 'Some naughty children did it. A disgraceful business,' and so saying he went over to the statues, set them to rights and walked off.

The holy man's tears of delight had been for nothing.

★

He whose deep love spurs him to dare all and go to his beloved, though 'watchful eyes surround the stealthy lover' and 'guards are set to snare him in the dark', will leave them both replete with powerful memories of all the moments when they tasted life's poignancy to the full. It must feel very awkward and unromantic for the woman, however, if a man simply takes her as his wife with the full consent of the family and without further ado.

How dreary it is when a woman hard up in the world announces that she will 'answer the call of any current' so long as he is well off, be it some unsuitable old priest or an uncouth Easterner, and a go-between sets about singing the praises of each to the other, with the result that she comes to someone's house as a bride without either knowing the other at all. What on earth would they say to each when they first come face to face? On the other hand, a couple can find endless conversation in the memories of long hardships overcome, 'forging their way through the dense autumn woods' to be together at last.

It can generally be said that a great deal of dissatisfaction results from a marriage set up by a third party. If the wife is excellent and the man a lowly and ugly old fellow, he will despise her for allowing herself to be thrown away on the likes of himself, and feel ashamed in her presence – a deplorable situation.

If you can never linger beneath the clouded moon on a plum-scented evening, nor find yourself recalling the dawns when you made your way home through the dew-soaked grasses by her gate after a night of love, you had best not aspire to be a lover at all.

★

The full moon's perfect roundness lasts barely a moment, and in no time is lost. Those with no eye for such things, it seems, fail to see how it changes in the course of a night.

An illness will grow graver as each moment passes, and death is already close at hand, yet while the sickness is still mild and you are not yet confronting death, you are lulled by your accustomed assumptions of a normal life in an unchanging world, and choose to wait until you have accomplished all you want in life before calmly turning your thoughts to salvation and a Buddhist practice, with the result that when you fall ill and confront death, none of your dreams has been fulfilled. Now, too late, you repent of your long years of negligence, and swear that if only you were to recover you would dedicate yourself unstintingly day and night to this thing and that – but for all your prayers your illness grows graver, until you lose your senses and die a raving death. It happens to so many of us. We must fully grasp this, here and now.

If you plan to turn your thoughts to the Buddhist Way after you have fulfilled all your desires, you will find that those desires are endless. What could be achieved, in this illusory life of ours? All desire is delusion. If desires arise within you, realize that they spring from your lost and deluded mind, and ignore them all. Relinquish all today and turn to the Buddhist path, and you will be freed of all obstruction, released from the need for action, and lasting peace will be yours body and soul.